C000230591

The Art of Poetry vol. 6

AQA: Power and Conflict

With special thanks to Matthew Curry, Michael Meally & Alex White.

Published by Peripeteia Press Ltd.

First published January 2017

ISBN: 978-0-9954671-2-5

Peripeteia.webs.com

Contents

General Introduction to the The Art of Poetry series

The philosopher Nietzsche described his work as 'the greatest gift that [mankind] has ever been given'. The Elizabethan poet Edmund Spenser hoped his book *The Faerie Queene* would magically transform its readers into noblemen. In comparison, our aims for *The Art of Poetry* series of books are a little more modest. Fundamentally we aim to provide books that will be of maximum use to English students and their teachers. In our experience, few students read essays on poems, yet, whatever specification they are studying, English students have to write analytical essays on poetry. So, we've offering some models, written in a lively and accessible style.

For Volume 1 we chose canonical poems for several reasons: Firstly, they are simply great poems, well worth reading and studying; secondly, we chose poems from across time so that they sketch in outline major developments in English poetry, from the Elizabethan period up until the present day, so that the volume works as an introduction to poetry and poetry criticism. And, being canonical poems, this selection often crops up on GCSE and A-level specifications, so our material will, we hope, be useful critical accompaniment and revision material. Our popular volumes 2-5 focused on poems set at A-level by the Edexcel and AQA boards respectively. In this current volume and its partner, volume 7, we turn our focus back to GCSE, providing critical support for students reading AQA's poetry anthology, and, in particular, those aiming to reach the very highest grades.

Introduction to *Volume 6:* Poems Past & Present, Power and Conflict

Power & Conflict

An adventure into what one apprehends

When writing about themes, students often simply state what they think the major theme of a poem to be. As AQA has kindly arranged these poems as a thematic cluster, writing something like 'this is a poem about power and conflict' doesn't get us very far. Sometimes readers also labour under a misconception about the nature of poetry, believing that poems have secret messages that poets annoyingly have hidden under deliberately obscure language. The task of the reader becomes to decode the obscure language and extract this buried message. Unsurprisingly, this misconception of poetry as a fancy subcategory of fables makes readers wonder why poets went to all the irritating trouble of hiding their messages in the first place. If they had something to say, why didn't the poet just say it and save everyone a lot of unnecessary fuss and bother? Why couldn't Browning, for instance, have just said that rich, powerful men can be abusive monsters?

The Romantic poet, John Keats's comment about distrusting poetry that has a 'palpable design' on the reader has been much quoted. For Keats, and many poets, a 'palpable design' is an aspect of rhetoric and particularly of propaganda and a poem is not just a piece of propaganda for a poet's ideas. As the modern poet, George Szirtes puts it, poems are not 'rhymed advertisements for the already formed views of poets'. Here's George discussing the issue: 'A proper poem has to be a surprise: no surprise for the poet no surprise for the reader, said Robert Frost and I think that he and Keats were essentially right. A proper poem should arise out of a naked unguarded experience that elicits surprise in the imagination by extending the consciousness in some way. Poetry is not what one knows but an adventure into what one apprehends.'[1]

Most poems are not merely prettified presentations of a poet's preformed views about a particular theme or issue; they are more like thought experiments or journeys of exploration and discovery. In other words, poetry, like all art, is equipment for thinking and feeling. So, instead of writing that 'poem x is about power and conflict' try to think more carefully through what is interesting or unusual or surprising about the poem's exploration of power and conflict. Sometimes the nature of the conflict or power play will be obvious, as in poems exploring warfare; at other times the conflicts might be more unusual or crop up in incongruous contexts. Sometimes the conflict may take the form of a psychological battle or the abuse of power take place in the context of social relationships, such as those between men and women or the wealthy and the poor. What does the poem have to say about its theme? What angle does the poet take? To what extent does the poem take up arms and argue for something and have a 'palpable design'? Is their attitude to the subject consistent or does it change? To what extent is the poem philosophical or emotional? Do we learn something new, does it change how we think or feel? How might the poem have extended our thinking?

It would be trite to conclude that all these various poems are merely telling us that conflict is a bad thing and that power is often abused. Conflict, after all, is an essential element to all dramatic art; the Greek 'agon' in protagonist and antagonist means conflict. Are there any poems in AQA's anthology celebrating conflict? Are there any instances of power in these poems being used constructively? Or are there any unusual or counterintuitive manifestations of power or conflict? The power of love? The power of empathy? The power of language? You get the idea. An adventure into what you apprehend is a great way to conceptualise a poem. And it's very productive too as a way to think about writing poetry criticism.

---

[1] http://georgeszirtes.blogspot.co.uk/

How to analyse a poem (seen or unseen)

A list of ingredients, not a recipe

Firstly, what not to do: sometimes pupils have been so programmed to spot poetic features such as alliteration that they start analysis of a poem with close reading of these micro details. This is never a good idea. A far better strategy is to begin by trying to develop an overall understanding of what the poem is about. Once this has been established, you can then delve into the poem's interior, examining its inner workings through the frame of your hypothesis. And you should be flexible enough to adapt, refine or even reject this hypothesis in the light of your investigation. The key thing is to make sure that whether you're discussing imagery or stanza form, sonic effects or syntax, enjambment or vocabulary, you always explore the significance of the feature in terms of meanings and effect.

Someone once compared texts to cakes. When you're presented with a cake the first thing you notice is what it looks like. Probably the next thing you'll do is taste it and find out if you like the flavour. This aesthetic experience will come first. Only later might you investigate the ingredients and how it was made. Adopting a uniform reading strategy is like a recipe; it sets out what you must, do step by step, in a predetermined order. This can be helpful, especially when you start reading and analysing poems. Hence in our first volume in *The Art of Poetry* series we explored each poem under the same subheadings of narrator, characters, imagery, patterns of sound, form & structure and contexts, and all our essays followed essentially the same direction. Of course, this is a reasonable strategy for reading poetry and will stand you in good stead. However, this present volume takes a different, more flexible approach, because this book is designed for students aiming for levels 7 to 9, or A to A* in old currency, and to reach the highest levels your work needs to be a bit more conceptual, critical and individual. AQA's assessment objectives for this paper, for instance, emphasise the need for 'critical' and 'exploratory' engagement with the poems. Top grade responses will also include 'fine-grained analysis of language, form and structure' informed by a 'conceptualised approach'.

Read our essays and you'll find that they all include the same principle ingredients – detailed, 'fine-grained' reading of crucial elements of poetry, imagery, form, rhyme and so forth - but each essay starts in a different way and each one has a slightly different focus or weight of attention on the various aspects that make up a poem. Once you have mastered the apprentice strategy of reading all poems in the same way, we recommend you put this generic essay recipe to one side and move on to a new approach, an approach that can change depending on the nature of the poem you're reading.

Follow your nose
Having established what you think a poem is about - its theme and what is interesting about the poet's treatment of the theme (the conceptual bit) - rather than then working through a pre-set agenda, decide what you honestly think are the most interesting aspects of the poem and start analysing these closely. This way your response will be original and you'll be writing about material you find most interesting. In other words, you're foregrounding yourself as an individual, critical reader. This most interesting aspect might be idea or technique based, or both. You might be most interested, for instance, in what Shelley suggests about the works of man, or you might be more interested in his use of the sonnet form, or how the latter contributes to the former. If, for you, the most intriguing aspect of Browning's *My Last Duchess* is how the poet manages the dramatic monologue form examine that. Or, if you notice how often words such as 'only', 'all one', 'all and each', 'alike', 'anybody' and 'the same' crop up in the poem and you think this is likely to be significant explore this feature and find out. Perhaps if you're reading Agard's poem you'll be captivated by how the poet rejects Standard English and creates as sense of a distinct spoken voice. Follow your own informed instincts, trust in yourself as a reader. If you're writing about material that genuinely interests you, your writing is likely to be interesting for your reader too.

Because of the focus on sonic effects and imagery other aspects of poems are often overlooked by students. It is a rare student, for instance, who notices how punctuation works in a poem and who can write about it convincingly. Few students write about the contribution of the unshowy function words, such as pronouns, prepositions or conjunctions, yet these words are crucial to any text. Of course, it would be a highly risky strategy to focus your whole essay on a seemingly innocuous and incidental detail of a poem. But noticing what others do not and coming at things from an unusual angle are as important to writing great essays as they are to the production of great poetry.

So, in summary when reading a poem have a check list in mind, but don't feel you must follow someone else's generic essay recipe. Consider the significance of major features, such as imagery, sonic patterns and form. Try to write about these aspects in terms of their contribution to themes and effects. But also follow your own nose, find your own direction, seek out aspects that genuinely engage you and write about these. The essays in this volume provide examples and we hope they will encourage you to go your own way at least to some extent and to make discoveries for yourself. No single essay could possibly cover everything that could be said about any one of these poems; aiming to create comprehensive essays like this would be foolish. And we have not tried to do so. Nor are our essays meant to be models for exam essays – they're far too long for that. They do, however, illustrate the sort of conceptualised, critical and 'fine-grained' exploration demanded for top grades at GCSE and beyond. There's always more to be discovered, more to say, space in other words for you to develop some original reading of your own.

Writing comparative essays

The following is adapted from our discussion of this topic in *The Art of Writing English Literature Essay*s A-level course companion, and is a briefer version, tailored to the GCSE exam task. Fundamentally comparative essays want you to display not only your ability to intelligently talk about literary texts, but also your ability to make meaningful connections between them. The first starting point is your topic. This must be broad enough to allow substantial thematic overlapping of the texts. However, too little overlap and it will be difficult to connect the texts; too much overlap and your discussion will be lopsided and one-dimensional. In the case of the GCSE exam, the broad topic will, of course, be conflict and power. The exam question will ask you to focus on the methods used by the poets to explore a specific theme. You will also be directed to write specifically on themes, language and imagery as well as other poetic techniques.

One poem from the anthology will be specified and printed on the paper. You will then have to choose a companion poem. Selecting the right poem for interesting comparison is obviously very important. Obviously, you should prepare for this task beforehand by pairing up the poems (a grid to aid this preparation can be found at the back of this book). To think about this task visually, you don't want Option A, below, [not enough overlap] or Option B [two much overlap]. You want Option C. This option allows substantial common links to be built between your chosen texts where discussion arises from both fundamental similarities AND differences.

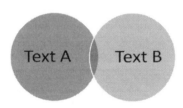

Option A: too many differences

Option B: too many similarities

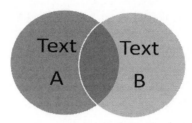

Option C: suitable number of similarities and differences

The final option will generate the most interesting discussion as it will allow substantial similarities to emerge as well as differences. The best comparative essays actually find that what seemed like clear similarities become subtle differences and vice versa while still managing to find rock solid similarities to build their foundations on.

Check the mark scheme for this question and you'll notice that to reach the top grade your comparison must be 'well-structured'. How should you structure a comparative essay? Consider the following alternatives. Which one is best and why?

Essay Structure #1
1. Introduction
2. Main body paragraph #1 - Text A
3. Main body paragraph #2 - Text A

4. Main body paragraph #3 - Text B
5. Main body paragraph #4 - Text B
6. Conclusion

Essay Structure #2

1. Introduction
2. Main body paragraph #1 - Text A
3. Main body paragraph #2 - Text A
4. Main body paragraph #3 - Text B
5. Main ody paragraph #4 - Text B
6. Comparison of main body paragraphs #1 & #3 - Text A + B
7. Comparison of main body paragraphs #2 & #4 - Text A + B
8. Conclusion

Essay Structure #3

1. Introduction
2. Main body paragraph #1 - Text A + B
3. Main body paragraph #2 - Text A + B
4. Main body paragraph #3 - Text A + B
5. Main body paragraph #4 - Text A+ B
6. Conclusion

We hope you will agree that 3 is the optimum option. Option 1 is the dreaded 'here is everything I know about text A, followed by everything I know by Text B' approach where the examiner has to work out what the connections are between the texts. This will score the lowest marks. Option 2 is better: There is some attempt to compare the two texts. However, it is a very inefficient way of comparing the two texts. For comparative essay writing the most important thing is to discuss both texts together. This is the most effective and efficient way of achieving your overall aim. Option 3 does this by comparing and contrasting the two texts under common umbrella headings. This naturally encourages comparison. Using comparative discourse markers, such as 'similarly', 'in contrast to', 'conversely' 'likewise' and 'however' also facilitates effective comparison.

When writing about each poem, make sure you do not work chronologically through a poem, summarising the content of each stanza. Responses of this sort typically start with 'In the first stanza' and employ discourse markers of time rather than comparison, such as 'after', 'next', 'then' and so forth. Even if your reading is analytical rather than summative, your essay should not work through the poem from the opening to the ending. Instead, make sure you write about the ideas explored in both texts (themes), the feelings and effects generated and the techniques the poets utilise to achieve these.

Writing about language

Poems are paintings as well as windows; we look at them as well as through them. As you know, special attention should be paid to language in poetry because of all the literary art forms poetry, in particular, employs language in a precise, self-conscious and distinctive way. Ideally in poetry, every word should count. Analysis of language falls into distinct categories:

- By diction we mean the vocabulary used in a poem. A poem might be composed from the ordinary language of everyday speech or it might use elaborate, technical or elevated phrasing. Or both. At one time some words and types of words were considered inappropriate for the rarefied field of poetry. The great Irish poet, W. B. Yeats never referred to modern technology in his poetry, there are no cars, or tractors or telephones, because he did not consider such things fitting for poetry. When much later, Philip Larkin used swear words in his otherwise well-mannered verse the effect was deeply shocking. Modern poets have pretty much dispensed with the idea of there being an elevated literary language appropriate for poetry. Hence in the AQA anthology you'll find all sorts of modern, everyday language, including some forthright swearing.

- Grammatically a poem may use complex or simple sentences [the key to which is the conjunctions]; it might employ a wash of adjectives and adverbs, or it may rely extensively on the bare force of nouns and verbs. Picking out and exploring words from specific grammatical classes has the merit of being both incisive and usually illuminating.

- Poets might mix together different types, conventions and registers of language, moving, for example, between formal and informal, spoken and written, modern and archaic, and so forth. Arranging the diction in the poem in terms of lexico-semantic fields, by register or by etymology, helps reveal underlying patterns of meaning.

- For almost all poems imagery is a crucial aspect of language. Broadly imagery is a synonym for description and can be broken down into two types, sensory and figurative. Sensory imagery means the words and phrases that appeal to our senses, to touch and taste, hearing, smell and sight. Sensory imagery is evocative; it helps to take us into the world of the poem to share the experience being described. Figurative imagery, in particular, is always significant. As we have mentioned, not all poems rely on metaphors and similes; these devices are only part of a poet's box of tricks, but figurative language is always important when it occurs because it compresses multiple meanings into itself. To use a technical term figurative images are polysemic - they contain many meanings. Try writing out the all the meanings contained in a metaphor in a more concise and economical way. Even simple, everyday metaphors compress meaning. If we want to say our teacher is fierce and powerful and that we fear his or her wrath, we can more concisely say our teacher is a dragon.

Writing about patterns of sound

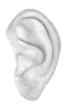 Like painters, some poets have powerful visual imaginations, while other poets have stronger auditory imaginations are more like musicians. And some poems are like paintings, others are more like pieces of music.

Firstly, what not to do: Tempting as it may be to spot sonic features of a poem and list these, don't do this. Avoid something along the lines of 'The poet uses alliteration here and the rhyme scheme is ABABCDCDEFEFGG'. Sometimes, indeed, it may be tempting to set out the poem's whole rhyme scheme like this. Resist the temptation: This sort of identification of features is worth zero marks. Marks in exams are reserved for attempts to link techniques to meanings and to effects.

Probably many of us have been sitting in English lessons listening somewhat sceptically as our English teacher explains the surprisingly specific significance of a seemingly random piece of alliteration in a poem. Something along the lines 'The double d sounds here reinforce a sense of invincible strength' or 'the harsh repetition of the 't' sounds suggests anger'. Through all our minds at some point may have passed the idea that, in these instances, English teachers appear to be using some sort of Enigma-style secret symbolic decoding machine that reveals how particular patterns of sounds have such definite encoded meanings.

And this sort of thing is not all nonsense. Originally deriving from an oral tradition, poems are, of course, written for the ear as much as for the eye, to be heard as much as read. A poem is a soundscape as much as it is a set of meanings. Sounds are, however, difficult to tie to very definite meanings and effects. By way of example, the old BBC Radiophonic workshop, which produced ambient sounds for radio and television programmes, used the same sounds in different contexts, knowing that the audience would perceive them in the appropriate way because of that context. Hence the sound of bacon sizzling, of an audience clapping and of feet walking over gravel were actually recordings of an identical sound. Listeners heard them differently because of the context. So, we may, indeed, be able to spot the repeated 's' sounds in a poem, but whether this creates a hissing sound, yes like a snake, or the susurration of the sea will depend on the context within the poem and the ears of the reader. Whether a sound is soft and soothing or harsh and grating is also open to interpretation.

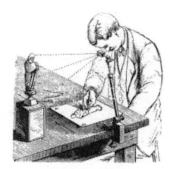

The idea of connecting these sounds to meanings or significance is a productive one. And your analysis will be most convincing if you use several pieces of evidence together. In other words, rather than try to pick out individual examples of sonic effects we recommend you explore the weave or pattern of sounds, the effects these generate and their contribution to feelings and ideas. For example, this might mean examining how alliteration and assonance are used together to achieve a particular mimetic effect.

Tennyson's *The Charge of the Light* Brigade is an especially noisy poem. In the central section the light brigade charge into a valley and are surrounded by cannons. Tennyson renders it thus:

'**Can**nons to the **right** of **them**
Cannons to the **left** of **them**
Cannons in **front** of **them**'

The sonic qualities of the word 'cannon' are emphasised through repetition at the start of each quick, short trimeter. The pacey effect is enhanced by a series of quick, short monosyllables which follow in each of the first three lines. Hence the verse skips speedily over unstressed syllables to hit the stressed ones (in bold) more emphatically. On top of this, the heavy 'em' end sound echoes the 'on' of 'cannon'. The overall effect is mimetic of cannon fire.

14

Writing about form & structure

As you know, there are no marks for simply identifying textual features. This holds true for language, sounds and also for form. Consider instead the relationship between a poem's form and its content, themes and effects. Form is not merely decorative or ornamental: A poem's meanings and effects are generated through the interplay of form and content. Broadly speaking the form can either work with or against a poem's content. Conventionally a sonnet, for instance, is about love, whereas a limerick is a comic form. A serious love poem in the form of a limerick would be unusual, as would a sonnet about an old man with a beard.

Sometimes poetic form can create an ironic backdrop to highlight an aspect of content. An example would be a formally elegant poem about something

monstrous. Browning's *My Last Duchess* springs to mind. The artist Grayson Perry uses form in this ironic way. Rather than depicting the sort of picturesque, idealised images we expect of ceramics, Perry's pots and urns depict modern life in bright, garish colours. The urn pictured, for instance, is entitled Modern Family and depicts two gay men with a boy who they have presumably adopted. A thrash metal concert inside a church, a philosophical essay via text message, a fine crystal goblet filled with cherryade would be further examples of ironic relationships between message and medium, content and context or form.

****

Reading form

Put a poem before your eyes. Start off taking a panoramic perspective: Think of the forest, not the trees. Perhaps mist over your eyes a bit. Don't even read the words, just look at the poem on the page, like at a painting. Is the poem slight, thin, fat, long, short? What is the relation of whiteness to blackness? Why might the poet have chosen this shape? Does it look regular or irregular? A poem about a long winding river will probably look rather different from one about a small pebble, or should do. Unless form is being employed ironically. Now read the poem a couple of times. First time, fast as you can, second time more slowly and carefully. How does the visual layout of the poem relate to what it seems to be about? Does this form support, or create a tension against, the content? Is the form one you can recognise, like a sonnet, or is it, perhaps, more open, more irregular like free verse? Usually the latter is obvious from the irregularity of the stanzas, line lengths and the lack of metre or rhyme.

As Hurley and O'Neill explain in *Poetic Form: An Introduction*, like genre, form sets expectations: 'In choosing form, poets bring into play associations and expectations which they may then satisfy, modify or subvert'.[2] We've already suggested that if we see a poem is a sonnet or a limerick this recognition will set up expectations about the nature of the poem's content. The same thing works on a smaller level; once we have noticed that a poem's first stanza is a quatrain, we expect it to continue in this neat, orderly fashion. If the quatrain's rhyme scheme is xaxa, xbxb, in which only the second and fourth lines rhyme, we reasonably expect that the next stanza will be xcxc. So, if it isn't we need to consider why.

After taking in the big picture in terms of choice of form in relation to content zoom in: Explore the stanza form, lineation, punctuation, the use of enjambment and caesura. Single line stanzas draw attention to themselves. If they are end-stopped they can suggest isolation, separation. Couplets imply twoness. Stanzas of three lines are called tercets and feature in villanelles and terza rima. On the page, both these forms tend to look rather delicate, especially if separated from each other by the silence of white space. Often balanced through rhyme, quatrains look a bit more robust and sturdy. Cinquains are swollen quatrains in which the last line often seems to throw

---

[2] Hurley & O'Neill, *Poetic Form, An Introduction*, p.3

the stanza out of balance.

Focus in on specific examples and on points of transition. For instance, if a poem has four regular quatrains followed by a couplet, examine the effect of this change. If we've been ticking along nicely in iambic metre and suddenly trip on a trochee, examine why. Consider regularity. Closed forms of poems, such as sonnets, are highly regular with set rhyme schemes, metre and number of lines. The opposite form is called 'open', the most extreme version of which is free verse. In free verse poems, the poet dispenses with any set metre, rhyme scheme or recognisable traditional form. What stops this sort of poetry from being prose chopped up to look like verse? The care of the design on the page. Hence, we need to focus here on lineation. Enjambment runs over lines and makes connections; caesura pauses a line and separates words. Lots of enjambment generates a sense of the language running away from the speaker. Lots of caesuras generate a halting, hesitant, choppy movement to lines. Opposites, these devices work in tandem and where they fall is always significant in a good poem.

Remember poetic form is never merely decorative. And bear in mind too the fact that the most volatile materials require the strongest containers.

Nice to metre...
A brief guide to metre and rhythm in poetry

Why express yourself in poetry? Why read words dressed up and expressed as a poem? What can you get from poetry that you can't from prose? There are many compelling answers to these questions. Here, though, we're going to concentrate on one aspect of the unique appeal of poetry – the structure of sound in poetry. Whatever our stage of education, we are all already sophisticated at detecting and using structured sound. Try reading the following sentences without any variation whatsoever in how each sound is  emphasised, and they will quickly lose what essential human characteristics they have. The sentences will sound robotic. So, in a sense, we won't be teaching anything new here. It's just that in poetry the structure of sound is carefully unusually crafted and created. It becomes a key part of what a poem is.

We will introduce a few new key technical terms along the way, but the ideas are straightforward. Individual sounds [syllables] are either stressed [emphasised, sounding louder and longer] or unstressed. As well as clustering into words and sentences for meaning, these sounds [syllables] cluster into rhythmic groups or feet, producing the poem's metre, which is the characteristic way its rhythm works.

In some poems, the rhythm is very regular and may even have a name, such as iambic pentameter. At the other extreme a poem may have no discernible regularity at all. As we have said, this is called free verse. It is vital to remember that the sound in a good poem is structured so that it combines effectively with the meanings.

For example, take a look at these two lines from Marvell's *To his Coy Mistress*:

'But at my back I alwaies hear
Times winged Chariot hurrying near:'

Forgetting the rhythms for a moment, Marvell is basically saying at this point 'Life is short, Time flies, and it's after us'. Now concentrate on the rhythm of his words.

- In the first line every other syllable is stressed: 'at', 'back', 'al', 'hear'.
- Each syllable before these is unstressed 'But', 'my', 'I', 'aies'.
- This is a regular beat or rhythm which we could write
  ti TUM / ti TUM / ti TUM / ti TUM , with the / separating the feet. ['Feet' is the technical term for metrical units of sound]
- This type of two beat metrical pattern is called iambic, and because there are four feet in the line, it is tetrameter. So this line is in 'iambic tetrameter'. [Tetra is Greek for four]
- Notice that 'my' and 'I' being unstressed diminishes the speaker, and we are already prepared for what is at his 'back', what he can 'hear' to be bigger than him, since these sounds are stressed.
- On the next line, the iambic rhythm is immediately broken off, since the next line hits us with two consecutive stressed syllables straight off: 'Times' 'wing'. Because a pattern had been established, when it suddenly changes the reader feels it, the words feel crammed together more urgently, the beats of the rhythm are closer, some little parcels of time have gone missing.

A physical rhythmic sensation is created of time slipping away, running out. This subtle sensation is enhanced by the stress-unstress-unstress pattern of words that follow, 'chariot hurrying' [TUM-ti-ti, TUM-ti-ti]. So the hurrying sounds underscore the meaning of the words.

14 ways of looking at a poem

Though conceived as pre-reading exercises, most of these tasks work just as well for revision.

1. Crunch it [1] – This means re-ordering all the text in the poem under grammatical headings of nouns, verbs, prepositions and so forth. If this is done before reading the poem for the first time, the students' task is [a] to try to create a poem from this material and [b] to work out what they can about the style and themes of the original poem from these dislocated grammatical aspects. An alternative is to list the words alphabetically and do same exercise. Re-arranging the poem in grammatical categories after reading can also be a useful analytical task.

2. Crunch it [2] – This is another exercise that can be used as an introductory activity before reading a poem for the first time, or as a useful revision task. Rearrange the poem into a list based on lexico-semantic fields. Show students one list of words at a time, asking them to write down what each group of words might tell us about the poem's themes & style. Alternatively, split the class into small groups and give each group one of the word lists. The groups work initially independently to work out what they can about the poem and then feed in their discoveries to the class. Once all the groups have shared their findings discuss what they can now predict about the poem. Ask each group to suggest a title for the poem. Compare.

3. Crunch it [3] – In this method students should reduce each line of the poem to one key word. If they do this individually, then in pairs, then as a class, it can facilitate illuminating whole class discussion and bring out different readings. We've applied this model of cruncher at the end of each of our essays.

4. Cloze it [aka blankety-blank] – A cloze exercise helps students to focus on specific choices of vocabulary. Blank out a few important words in the first couple of stanzas and as much as you dare of the rest of the poem. Make this task harder as the course goes on. Or use it for revision to see how well the poem's been remembered.

5. Shuffle it – Give students all the lines in the poem but in the wrong order. Their task is to find the right order. Make this a physical exercise; even older pupils like sticking cut up pieces of paper together! Start off with reasonably easy activities. Then make them fiendishly hard.

6. Split it – Before a first reading, post a few key lines from the poem around the classroom, like clues for literary detectives. Arrange the class into small groups. Each group analyses only a few lines. Feedback to the class what they have found out, what they can determine about the poem. Ask them how the information from other groups confirms/ changes their thoughts. Finish by getting them to sequence the lines.

7. Transform it – Turn the poem into something else, a storyboard for a film version, a piece of music or drama, a still image, a collage of images a piece of performance art. Engage your and their creativity.

8. Switch it – Swap any reference to gender in the poem and the gender of the poet. Or change every verb or noun or metaphor or smile in the poem. Compare with the non-doctored version; what's revealed?

9. Pastiche or parody it – Ask students to write a poem in the style of one of the poems from the anthology. Impose a strict rule that the students must not share their poems with each other before class. Take printed copies in. Add your own and one other poem. See if the students can recognise the published poem from the imitations. A points system can add to the fun.

10. Match it [1] – Ask students to find an analogue for the poem. Encourage them to think metaphorically. If they think poem x is like a thrash metal song by The Frenzied Parsnips they'll really need to explain how.

11. Match it [2] – Take some critical material on about 5 or 6 poets; there's good stuff on the Poetry by Heart and Poetry Archive websites. Take one poem by each of these poets and a photo. Mix this material up on one page of A3. The students' task is to match the poet to the critical material and to the image. To add to the creativity, make up a poem, poet and critical comments. See if they can spot the fake.

12. Complete it - Give the students the first few lines of the poem. Their task is to complete it. If they get stuck and plead profusely, and if you're feeling especially generous, drop in a few clues from time to time, such as the rhyme scheme or the stanza form.

13. Write back to - If the poem's a dramatic monologue, change the point of view and write the other character's version of events. What might be the silent thoughts of the messenger in *My Last Duchess*? What might the Agard's teachers say if they could reply to his poem?

14. Listen to it – Poems are designed for the ear as much as for the eye. Tell the class you're going to read the poem once. Their task is to listen especially carefully and then write down as much of it as they can remember, working first on their own and then in pairs. Read the poem a second time and repeat the exercise. Discuss what they did and didn't remember. Why did some bits stick in the ear?

'Poetry is a verdict that others give to language that is charged with music and rhythm and authority.'

LEONARD COHEN

William Blake, *London*

The first thing to notice about Blake's poem is its burning anger. Written over two hundred years ago, the nightmare vision of this poem still seems irradiated with the poet's righteous fury. Fury at the corruption London's inhabitants had to endure, fury at the powers maintaining and enforcing this corruption. And who or what is to blame for the universal corruption? Blake is characteristically direct and bold: The finger of blame is pointed at commerce, the church and the monarchy.

Land and water in this poem have both been 'chartered', an adjective that indicates that they have become property, to be bought and sold by chartered companies. However, Blake subtly implies a potential counter force; the verb 'flows', with its slight echo of 'wander', perhaps implies that the river at least has the potential to escape its commercial restriction. For Blake, the Church was part of a corrupt, oppressive state. Here the churches are 'black'ning' because they should be an active voice of protest against the exploitation of children. The failure of the church blackens its name as well as its bricks. The blood of the soldier runs down the palace walls, a gruesome symbol of the sacrifice the ordinary man makes for King and country.

Every voice

Repetition is a key poetic device for all poets, but it is especially important for Blake. It can fall into a few different categories: diction (or vocabulary); syntax (word order); images; sounds.

- In *London* there are lots of 'ins', 'ands', 'everys' as well as 'chartered', 'marks' and 'cry'.
- As well as repetition of single words there is repetition of syntax: 'in every...in every...in every'.
- Sound patterns are also repeated, such as in 'marks of weakness, marks of woe', 'mind-forg'd manacles', 'most through midnight', 'blasts' and 'blights'.
- Most importantly images are also repeated: The images of the chimney sweep, the soldier and the prostitute are three versions of the same figure; the character marginalized and exploited by society.

As well as creating rhetorical emphasis and a powerful rhythmical charge, reminiscent of spells and incantations, such insistent repetition creates an almost claustrophobic sound world, one that is an aural equivalent of the oppression Blake is describing.

The poem's rhyme scheme is cross-rhyme in quatrains: ABAB, CDCD and so forth. All the rhymes are masculine, a choice that also contributes to the peculiar intensity of the poem. For example, in the fourth line the stress starts with a strong stress on 'marks' and ends with another strong stress on 'woe'. Each stanza constitutes one sentence, completed in its final emphatic monosyllable. Metre, rhyme, diction, lineation and syntax all work together to amass maximum weight and stress on these last key words, 'woe', 'hear', 'walls' and finally, of course, 'hearse'.

The poem comprises four stanzas of four lines (quatrains) each with four beats. This consistency creates a concentration, further adding to its power. Structurally the poem also increases in intensity, as we move from verbs such as 'flow' and 'mark' in the first stanza to the more powerful emphatic 'curse', 'blasts' and 'blights' in the final stanza. As we go on to examine, this pattern is re-enforced by the increasingly poignant examples of exploitation, from the general populace to the chimney sweeper to the 'youthful harlot' whose curse Blake hears 'most'.

The dark mark

As in fellow poet William Wordsworth's famous 'I wander lonely as a cloud', 'wander' is a form of motion particularly associated with Romanticism. Wandering suggests freedom, finding one's own path, without any specific aim in mind. It may also imply a sense of being lost. In Blake's poem, the verb emphasizes the idea that exploitation in London is universal; the poet doesn't have to search for it, whatever direction he takes he's sure to find it. Though they are in the active voice, the verbs connected to the narrator – 'wander', 'mark', 'hear' - suggest that Blake is passive and perhaps powerless. Rather than an active participant in the world of the poem who can make things happen, he is an outsider, a witness, registering his impressions as vividly as he can. Perhaps this is the role of the artist.

However, look at the line: 'and mark in every face I meet/ marks of weakness, marks of woe'. 'Mark' is used here first as a verb and then as a noun, and is a word connecting the narrator to the suffering people. Blake could easily have chosen a different verb. He was an engraver as well as a poet and to engrave the pictures that accompanied the poems in *Songs of Innocence and Experience* he would have had to cut into metal. Compared to 'see' or 'notice', 'mark' signals permanence. It also implies something doomed, as in the mark of Cain, or for Harry Potter fans the 'dark mark'. The fact that the poet 'marks' the people's 'marks' implies an equality and connection between them. If he is an outsider, he's an insider too, expressing a radical sympathy with the suffering he sees.

Repetition of the adjective 'every' emphasizes Blake's idea that every human being matters. The crowd represents the ordinary masses, the common people, whose suffering is often ignored by those in power. Over in France, Europe's leaders had witnessed the first 'successful' rebellion of the commoners in history. The British government responded with a harsh crackdown on freedom. Romantic poets often sided with people marginalised by society or oppressed by authority; Blake's poem protests against the malign effects of power on those at the bottom of society. The soldier, sweep and prostitute are emblems of exploitation: The sweep would have been a young boy sold into a form of slavery (see Blake's two Chimney Sweeper poems in *Songs of Innocence and Experience*). Abused and brutalised, sweeps were regarded at this time as the lowest form of human life, on a par with 'savages' who shared their black skin. The soldier's blood is used to protect the state and the monarchy. The prostitute is, however, an example of the worst possible exploitation. Blake believed love to be sacred. Turning sex and love into a commodity to be bought and sold was therefore a sin against God, the most heinous form of sacrilege.

This is a poem full of aural as well as visual imagery: The voices of the Londoners, the clink of their mental manacles, the cries of the sweepers, the cursing of the prostitute. For Romantic Poets, such as Blake, nature was sacred. Nature manifested God on earth and was a great source of poetic inspiration. This unhappy, discordant, diseased, corrupted city is the nightmare opposite of Eden. The image of the soldier's 'sigh'

running in 'blood down palace walls' combines sound with sight. It is extraordinary in two ways: firstly, Blake transforms sound, a 'sigh', into something visual. The synaesthetic effect generated has a nightmarish quality; secondly, as we have already noted, he bravely points directs the blame at the King. This was a very dangerous thing to say in England in 1792, in a time when some of Blake's fellow radicals were being arrested by the government and attacked by pro monarchy gangs. The penalties for treason were very severe.

Thought control

The 'mind forg'd manacles' is one of Blake's most celebrated images. It is characteristically Blakean because it conveys an idea (here of being  brainwashed) in a concrete, physical image. The image of the manacles is one of mental chains, thought control, indoctrination. The poet does not indicate who forges these manacles. It could be that they are made by the state through propaganda. But they could also be formed in the minds of individuals, in their blinkered perceptions and ways of seeing the world. In either case, there is hope - these aren't real chains; they are 'mind forg'd' and perceptions can be changed, perhaps by poetry. 'Forg'd' is a doubly appropriate verb: An image drawn from metal work, it is a pun. These perceptions of reality are forgeries, forgeries that can and must be exposed by the sort of truth articulated in this poem.

Arguably, however, the poem's most potent image is the final one. Notice how the structure of the poem develops in a cinematic fashion. Starting with the equivalent of an establishing shot - a wide-angle image of the landscape, the focus narrows to a closer in inspection of the crowds, and finishes with a shot of a single emblematic figure. Like a film camera we sweep the whole scene then zoom in as day darkens to night, before finishing, seemingly inevitably at the apex of exploitation, the moral midnight of the 'youthful harlot'.

Blake employs an image of sexual infection as a metaphor for moral corruption. Disease spreads through time and space: It will be spread through the generations, from the prostitute to her child; spread from prostitute to client, and spread into marriage, the home, the family. The deadly destruction this process will wreak is conveyed by those violent plosive & alliterative verbs 'blasts' and the biblical 'blights', and through the similarly biblical word 'plagues'. Plagues also suggests disease and especially the deadly Black Plague. Hence Blake evokes the image of God's punishment of sin. As the image of the charming plague doctor at the start of this essay suggests, it's like something out of *Night of the Living Dead.* Corruption so potent can, indeed, even transform a celebration of new life into an image of death, as in the startling oxymoron of the 'marriage hearse'.

Songs of Innocence and Experience

London is from *Songs of Experience* (1792), the companion piece to his

earlier *Songs of Innocence.* Blake was an idealist who wanted to see a better, fairer world. The front covers signal the different tones of the two books; where the Innocence image is maternal and comforting, the Experience images is sombre and suggests mourning for a spiritual loss. In many of the Experience poems Blake analyses and criticizes the harsh values of his society. Throughout the collection, he protests against injustice and exploitation. He stands up as a champion of the poor and challenges the cruelty of those in power. In this enterprise,

Blake's spiritual guide was Christ who he called 'Jesus, the imagination'.

Blake was an artist as well as a poet and his illustrations were an integral part of his poems. Many of the illustrations accompanying the *Innocence* poems are rich, boldly coloured, sensual designs, presenting children playing in harmonious relation within exuberantly fertile images of nature. In contrast the palette of the *Experience* is much narrower and gloomier, conjuring a shadow world, drained of colour, dominated by greys and blacks.

The characters in these images express suffering and misery. Boxed in by the borders of the page, they appear trapped in their oppressive worlds. It is interesting that Blake depicts himself as two figures in the illustration to *London*. He is both the angelic child guide and the old man lead through the circles of this particular depiction of hell. In other words, he is both innocence and experience. Significantly at the end of the poem the image of innocence has disappeared.

An age of revolutions

Blake's *Songs of Innocence* poems generally focus on childhood and are celebratory and optimistic in tone; the 'Experience' poems are much angrier. This darkening of mood between the two may have been due to Blake's reaction to the French Revolution of 1789. Like other Romantic poets, initially Blake saw the revolution as a great uprising of the human spirit, a liberation of the masses from the corrupt and unjust powers of the State. But as time went on news filtered through to England of appalling massacres carried out by the revolutionary forces. Over time it was becoming apparent that the French Revolution would result in one form of tyranny, that of the Monarchy, being replaced by another, that of the Masses.

London crunched

Crunching a poem entails choosing what you consider to be the most significant word in each line. If a whole class, working individually, crunches a poem, comparing the decisions made can be a very useful exercise. Before you read our crunch of Blake's poem, have a go yourself. And then compare. Did we agree about the most important words?

Wander – chartered – mark – woe – every – cry – every – manacles – chimney-sweeper – church – soldier – palace – midnight – harlot – new-born – hearse.

William Wordsworth, *Extract from, The Prelude*

It is easy to understand why poems such as *Bayonet Charge* and *Kamikaze* were selected for an anthology of poetry about conflict, but, on first reading, we might question the inclusion of the extract from *The Prelude*, which describes a young boy rowing a boat out into the middle of a lake and then returning; the potential for conflict seems limited. Even in *Storm on the Island* - another poem overtly about nature - we can comprehend how conflict manifests itself in the tempest that batters the island. But in *The Prelude,* nature does not actually change or do anything. However, what does change is the speaker's perception of nature, which leads to a disturbing transfer of power from the boy in the first half of the poem onto the natural world in the second half. Rather than a conflict that takes place externally in the outside world between people, the conflict of *The Prelude* extract is an internal one that takes place within the mind and emotions of the individual speaker.

Before we take a closer look at how the poem works, it is useful to reflect on the poem's context, form and structure. Wordsworth was one of the leading poets of the Romantic movement of the nineteenth century, an artistic and philosophical movement that sought to explore and explain the individual and his/her relationship to society and the natural world though the power of emotions and the imagination, rather than through rational and scientific enquiry. In particular, the Romantics saw the imagination and its interplay with nature as the key to attaining a deeper understanding of who we are and what the universe is really like, an insight which is central to understanding this extract from *The Prelude*.

When considering the poem's form and structure, it is also important to note that this extract is part of a much longer poem, *The Prelude or, Growth of a Poet's Mind*, which Wordsworth worked on for most of his adult life and which ran to almost eight thousand lines! Wordsworth had set out to write an epic poem to rival John Milton's monumental masterpiece, *Paradise Lost*. Epic poems are long narrative poems that explore historical or mythological events important to the culture in which they are written. Milton's poem traced the fall of Adam and Eve from the Garden of Eden into a world of sin and death; Wordsworth, in a turn of Romantic individualism, cast himself as the hero of his own epic and wrote *The Prelude* to examine the significant moments from his own life that had led him to becoming a poet and which had shaped his understanding of the world. However, like Milton, Wordsworth chose to compose his poem in blank verse, unrhymed lines of five stressed syllables usually with an iambic metre. This not only enabled Wordsworth to replicate the natural rhythms of everyday speech - a particular concern of the Romantic poets - but also gave him the flexibility to relate and unfold events for the reader in the naturalistic and organic way he actually experienced them, rather than distort experience by forcing it to conform to a strict rhyme scheme or inflexible metrical pattern.

One summer evening

The extract starts simply enough, with the young Wordsworth finding a small rowing boat moored by the side of a lake. The poet reveals that it was nature personified as a goddess or maternal force that led him to the boat, yet the parenthesis suggests this is the retrospective understanding of the older poet rather than an awareness of divine intervention - a characteristic trait of epic poetry - intuited by the young boy. In the second sentence, it is now the boat which is personified and feminised as the poet recalls how 'Straight I unloosed her chain, and stepping in/ Pushed from the shore'. The boy imagines himself almost as a heroic knight of Chivalric romance, liberating the helpless maiden in distress. There is no hesitancy in his actions; both lines start with a reversed metrical foot whereby the iambic pattern is substituted for a trochaic one so that the first syllables of each line 'Straight' and 'Pushed' are stressed. This creates a sense of urgency, confidence, forcefulness and determination to his actions. Urgency is further emphasised by the enjambment of 'and stepping in/ Pushed', which leaves little time to question the moral implications of taking the boat without permission. If the boy did pause to consider what the older poet recognizes as 'an act of stealth/ And troubled pleasure', it is quickly passed over as he rows the boat out onto the lake and witnesses 'on either side/ Small circles glittering idly in the moon /Until they melted all into one track/ Of sparkling light'. The scene is one of spectacular beauty where the ripples from the boy's oars reflect the moon's light and form a trail behind the boat where the heavens and the Earth seem to merge and become indistinguishable. Wordsworth's use of the present participles 'glittering' and  'sparkling' accentuates the immediacy of the experience and seem to bathe him in a celestial light, while the sense of being caught breathless by this moment of transcendent, heavenly vision is reproduced by his use of an expansive sentence that spans seven lines. The way in which the ripples from the oars melt 'into one track' is also suggestive of the workings of memory, where seemingly random and inexplicable moments from our present recede into the past to be given retrospectively a shape and purpose that provide meaning and direction to our lives - a fitting emblem of Wordsworth's purposes throughout *The Prelude*. It is perhaps not by chance that the word 'I' echoes through these lines in the assonance of 'side', 'idly' and 'light'.

As the boy continues to row out into the lake, his confidence - possibly even arrogance - in his own skill and strength is once again made evident. The poet notes how he is 'Proud of his skill' as he dips his oars 'lustily' into the waters. The adverb here suggests the delight he takes in his own power and energy which verges on sexual excitement. The present participle 'heaving' further

reinforces the sense of vigour and force, while the simile 'like a swan' reflects the boy's skilful and graceful mastery over the boat and the natural world embodied by the lake. Epic poetry typically depicts the heroic exploits of mythological warriors and the metaphorical transformation of the small rowing boat into 'an elfin pinnace' suggests the younger Wordsworth was casting himself in such a role, a 'pinnace' being a small boat with several sails that was part of a warship, with the adjective 'elfin' helping to create the atmosphere of mystical enchantment. However, it is in the boy's 'unswerving line' as he fixes his eyes upon 'The horizon's utmost boundary' where the Ozymandias-like sense of complete dominance over his environment is most apparent. It is as if through the imagination and sheer will-power the boy intends his heroic quest to take him through the boundaries of the known universe. Wordsworth seems to enact this shattering of limitations by extending this line to twelve syllables rather than the expected ten. However, the disruption this causes creates a jarring effect, hinting that the boy's sense of control over the natural world is not as comprehensive as he currently believes. It is his mistaken belief that 'far above/ Was nothing but the stars and the grey sky', the assumption that he comprehends everything within his environs, which leads to the shock and disempowerment that Wordsworth relates in the second half of the extract.

A huge peak, black and huge

The whole extract turns on the word 'when', which appears roughly in the middle of the remarkable sentence that begins 'She was...' in line seventeen and ends with 'Upreared its head' in line twenty-four. This sentence has already guided the reader through four lines of the boy's triumphant journey into the centre of the lake, but as the speaker moves out of the shadow of the 'craggy ridge' (it is important to understand that as he been rows the boat forwards into the lake he is actually facing back towards the shoreline) a higher peak behind the first now suddenly becomes visible. Wordsworth delays the all-important verb 'upreared' until the very end of this extremely lengthy sentence to build tension and suspense, but also to evoke the boy's own confusion and bewilderment as the mountain rises ominously into view. The force of the shock lies in the boy's false and overconfident assumption that the first 'ridge' was the boundary of the horizon, so that there could be nothing else behind it. Whether he recognizes in the rational part of his mind that this emerging shape is a mountain is irrelevant; what matters is that in his imagination this shape is transformed into an indefinable and overwhelming creature or sentient force that now strides after him like the giant in a fairy tale chasing down the young thief. However, there is no heroic response in this tale. Instead, the boy's sheer terror is captured in the frantic repetition of 'I struck and struck again' as he attempts to outrun the nightmarish entity. Yet the further away he rows, the larger and more overpowering the mountain becomes, giving the appearance that the 'grim shape' is pursuing him as if an avenging, supernatural creature out of Gothic fiction.

But what most terrifies the boy is the mountain's sheer otherness; whereas earlier in the extract Wordsworth had personified and feminized both nature and the boat, it is significant that here the mountain is described twice with the pronoun 'it'. He cannot subdue or familiarize it through the power of his imagination and the failure of language is registered in the repetition of 'a huge peak, black and huge', where the plain, uninspired and repetitive diction contrasts tellingly with the transcendent, highly poetic imagery deployed earlier in the poem. The boy is overwhelmed and his earlier confidence of mastery over the natural world is instantly destroyed. Instead, it is the mountain peak, and by extension, nature itself, which is filled with 'voluntary power' independent of mankind and infinitely more potent. What the boy discovers is that nature is not only beautiful but can also be sublime, evoking awe and terror at its uncontrollable power. It is this terror which is externalized onto the 'trembling oars' that propel the speaker back to the safety of the shore.

The final lines of the poem reflect on the significance of this life-changing experience. One thing the experience seems to have taught the boy is an awareness of moral culpability and guilt in the act of stealing the boat; the description of how he 'stole my way/ Back to the covert of the willow tree' draws attention to the act of theft not only through the verb 'stole', but also 'covert', which as a noun is another word for the 'cove' where he initially found the boat, but as an adjective carries the additional meaning of something done secretly. Repeated reference here to the 'willow tree' also highlights the associations of the tree with grief and sorrow, which implies an acceptance of guilt. On this reading, nature has acted like a stern parent, disciplining and correcting its child out of love, although this is something only understood by the poet as he reflects on what happened. This draws a parallel with Milton's rendering of Adam and Eve's story in *Paradise Lost* - the epic poem Wordsworth was consciously seeking to emulate - which also deals with the themes of pride, guilt, and divine correction.

Blank desertion

Yet there does seem to be more to this experience than just an acknowledgement of personal guilt. When Wordsworth notes how he returned home in 'grave/ And serious mood', we cannot help but hear the secondary meaning of 'grave' as a place of burial. It is possible the shock of encountering this unexplainable presence awoke in the poet an understanding of his own vulnerability, insignificance and mortality in the face of the great forces of nature which, as is clear in *Ozymandias*, will long outlast any assertions of human power. But what seems most troubling for Wordsworth is the sense of an existential crisis that the experience triggers, whereby the poet's understanding and ability to give meaning to the universe is suddenly shattered. The adjectives 'dim', 'undetermined' and 'unknown' all point to his inability to fit the experience into any of his preconceived notions and categories. When he writes 'call it solitude/ Or blank desertion' he is really admitting he has no words to describe what he felt and can only settle for vague approximations. Instead, he can only define the experience by what it was not, as is accentuated by the triple anaphoric phrases, 'No familiar shapes', 'no pleasant images' and 'no colours of green fields', which echoes Milton once again through reference to a paradise that is now lost. The images of natural beauty have been supplanted by the 'huge and mighty forms' that represent the incomprehensible and untameable power of nature that oppress and overwhelm the young Wordsworth. The extract ends with disillusionment and disempowerment as the boy discovers he is not the master of his own world. Yet in removing this youthful delusion the way is now cleared for a more measured and sober understanding of the world and the poet's place within it, something Wordsworth continues to work out over the course the entire poem of which this extract forms just one small but significant part.

The Prelude crunched:

Summer – boat – cove – unloosed – stealth troubled – mountain-echoes – her – moon – melted – sparkling – proud – fixed – summit – boundary – stars – lustily – dipped – boat – swan – behind – huge – power – struck – grim – towered – purpose – thing – trembling – stole – covert – left – homeward – mood – many – dim – unknown – darkness – desertion – no – no – mighty – mind – dreams.

Percy Bysshe Shelley, *Ozymandias*

Man vs. nature & time

In a sense, Shelley's poem has three narrators:

1. the author of the inscription
2. the first person voice
3. and words by or put in the mouth of the subject of the sculpture, Ozymandias aka the Egyptian Pharaoh Ramasses II.

The little piece of recorded speech is related by the traveller, and hence enclosed within the traveller's narration. And all that the traveller says is related to us by the first speaker, the poet, and so enclosed by the poet. This device of several enclosed narratives, rather like a Russian doll, means that Shelley can delineate the desert and the Pharaoh, their vastness and power, but at the same time control and enclose them as miniatures inside his field of powerful language, his poem.

The traveller from 'an antique land' provides an exotic element to the poem and an implied contrast with the poet's more limited experience. Romantic poets, such as Blake, Wordsworth and Shelley were drawn to solitary individuals who quested after knowledge, wisdom and understanding. This quest often took them to some sort of sublime natural environment, such as a mountain range or a desert. It is characteristic of the Romantics to find wisdom far away from civilisation and the comforts of home.

The Pharaoh, Ramasses, is an emblem of autocratic political power: 'the sneer of cold command'. He is presented as hubristic, i.e. so full of his own self-importance that he is due a fall. Arrogance and vanity are demonstrated by his having a statue erected to himself on which he has the extraordinarily vain and foolish words, 'king of kings' engraved. However magnificent and

indomitable Ramesses thought himself, Shelley shows, however, how puny his power was against the vast might of nature and of time. So, Shelley's poem warns tyrants that however impregnable their position may appear to be, they are in reality vulnerable. To less powerful, ordinary people this is a message of political hope.

The unnamed and unknown artist is a kindred spirit for the poet. Part of the poem's business is to assert and demonstrate the primacy and permanence of forms created by art over the more transient trappings of worldly power. Time, however, has changed the meaning of the statue, with the vainglorious inscription now resonating ironically against the blank emptiness of the desert.

The imagery gives the reader a sense of the exotic through the traveller, the antique land, and the extraordinary name, 'Ozymandias'. Shelley also includes images of desolation and destruction, such as the trunkless legs, shattered visage, decay, desert, sand and the wreck. Violence is also suggested generally through the wreckage, as well as specific verbs, such as 'shattered' and 'stamped'.

The scale of the statue is conveyed through the adjectives, 'vast' and 'colossal'. Yet this huge wreckage is dwarfed by the enormity of nature, here in its perhaps most desolate form, the desert. The adjectival phrase 'boundless and bare' implies the desert is both endless and endlessly featureless, a sense of an eternity of nothingness enhanced in the final line, 'the lone and level sands stretch away'. There is a suggestion here of the desert as time and the endless time of death.

Sounds in the desert

The sound 'and' occurs fifteen times. That's a lot for a fourteen line poem, and that repetition of sound, coupled with its sense of going on, of continuing, adding, helps give the poem its drive and momentum. Also the rhyme scheme, abab acdc edef ef holds the poem tightly together, giving the reader an impression of something unified and complete. Notice how the first rhyme 'land' is passed from the first four line stanza, or quatrain, to the second, 'command', the seventh rhyme, 'things' runs into the third quatrain, and the eighth, 'appear' continues into the final couplet. Internal rhyme of 'Round' and 'boundless' with the assonance of 'nothing', 'colossal' and 'lone' set up the finish by helping to slow and steady the reader. This change of tempo is reinforced by sonic qualities:

- the alliteration of 'boundless and bare' and 'lone and level'
- and the dominant drawn out long 'o' and 'ow' sounds.

One interesting syntactical device Shelley employs in this poem is the use of two adjectives connected by 'and': 'vast and trunkless', 'boundless and bare', 'lone and level'. These give the reader a sense of full and yet qualified description, a double vision of the object described. It's an economical technique that helps give us the impression of a real landscape the poet is capturing rather than creating.

Ozymandias is a sonnet, although as we saw above the rhyme scheme isn't traditional. There is no obvious break in the pattern where you might expect the volta, or 'turn'. The 'turn' is change in direction in a poem, a feature of traditional sonnets where, usually after the octave, there is a change or shift in emphasis or argument, or a new subject or angle is introduced. And indeed there is no turn in this sonnet. One thing that makes this poem so innovative is the way that instead of a neat argument, with a turn after line eight and a flourish at the end, as per a conventional sonnet, the structure here is one of enclosure: Three statements creating three little worlds within them. This delivers a tremendously powerful sense of unity, and allows the poet and the reader to play with and control scale in a seemingly effortless way.

Shelley is an expert at speeding up and slowing the reader down, so that the rhythm of the words underscores the meaning. The following two examples illustrate this point nicely:

- The line 'look on my words, ye Mighty, and despair' has only four stresses and so trips along quickly: TUM ti – ti TUM ti-TUM, ti- ti ti TUM
- This creates a contrast with the following half line which is much slower, 'Nothing beside remains', TUM-ti ti-TUM ti-TUM.

Even though almost all of this poem is reported speech, and natural enough sounding, it still fits the sonnet form, without seeming in any way forced. That shows considerable skill. And though the lines would sound wrong read as iambic pentameter, that rhythm is there as part of the poem's sonic substratum, its deep undersong.

Enjambment is the running of sentences over the line breaks; caesura is the splitting of lines with a pause. These two devices work together to run against the regular pattern of the rhyme scheme. They help to convey the sense of a speaking voice, making the words sound more natural by reducing the emphasis at the end of each line. Look at the end-stopped lines: They come at the end of the octave:

- line 8, '...and the heart that fed'
- line 11, '...and despair'
- and in the final level with its unequivocal full stop.

The effect is to lend greater emphasis to these particular rhyme words. The poem runs up in a long sentence to 'fed', a word that conveys how much the ordinary people relied on the 'heart', signifying emotions of the Pharaoh. Shelley wanted to emphasise 'despair' and 'away' for obvious reasons. The caesuras in the final lines are particularly effective. The pauses after 'nothing beside remains' and 'colossal wreck' allow the absoluteness of the phrases to sink in, as well as suggesting momentarily empty or emptied space.

Stretching far away...

Friend of Lord Byron and John Keats, husband of the writer of *Frankenstein*, Mary Shelley, Percey Bysshe Shelley was part of the second generation of Romantic poets which had followed the trail blazed by Blake, Wordsworth and

Coleridge. A political idealist, like Blake, Shelley expressed strongly anti-establishment views. Indeed, Shelley's views were so radical and incendiary that little of his work was published in his lifetime. Like Blake, Shelley was writing at a time of great political volatility in the turbulent years that followed the French Revolution.

In *Ozymandias* Shelley asserts the enduring power of art and artists over that of kings, pharaohs and in particular tyrants. Like other Romantics, Shelley also shows how the creations of man are made to seem minute when set against nature and the cosmic dimension of time. Nevertheless, unlike the statue it depicts, Shelley's poem looks set to endure.

Ozymandias crunched:

Obviously, this process will always be a personal one. This is just one possibility. Do it yourself and see where we agree and disagree. What have you spotted that we have not?

Antique – trunkless – desert – visage – sneer – sculptor – lifeless – mocked – pedestal – Ozymandias – despair – decay – wreck – sands.

(One sign of this poem's greatness is the fact that it could be 'crunched' in many interesting ways – every single word tells.)

Robert Browning, *My Last Duchess*

Can you recognise a monster when you see one? Why of course you can; it's an essential life skill. Monsters are huge and hairy with horrible warts on their faces; they have horns on their heads and terrible claws and mouths full of spikey teeth. Monsters have wings or scales and they hiss or growl, slobber or roar, and they slither around or they scuttle, crawl or lope. Basically, monsters are amalgams of all the features we find frightening or disgusting in the animal kingdom. In short, monsters always look something like the grumpy looking little critter on our right of this page:

Right?
Wrong.

And we know where to find monsters too: In horror films and fairy tales, in the middle of the woods, under our beds, hiding in our cupboards, in nightmares.

Right?
Wrong.

Because make no mistake about it, though he's a Duke and fabulously wealthy and lives in a fabulous mansion, though he's highly refined and speaks impressively and fluently, though he is a connoisseur of fine art and is exactingly polite, even though we find him here in the elegant frame of this poem, this character is a monster. And monsters who disguise their monstrosity under an attractive façade are the most scary and dangerous monsters, right? Right.

Browning's poem is a superlative example of a dramatic monologue, a poem written in the voice of a character. As the name implies, a dramatic monologue is like a single speech from a play. A successful dramatic monologue will not only allow an insight into the character speaking but also suggest a wider narrative of which they are part. A key technique in a dramatic monologue is irony. The irony operates in the gap between what the speaking character is telling us and what the writer is telling us about them. In Browning's poem, we have a number of characters - the Duke, the Duchess, the Count's messenger as well as the implied voice of the poet himself. The reader is placed in the position of the messenger to whom our narrator, the Duke, tells us a story about his dead wife.

What makes this poem superlative? Think for a moment of the technical challenge Browning has set himself. Creating the authentic voice of the Duke would be a stiff challenge for any novelist, using prose, but Browning has got to make this voice sound natural and convincing whilst stringing it across a regular metre. More than that, he has also chosen to use the couplet form, a form which inevitably draws attention to the rhyme words. Notice how Browning arranges sentences to subdue these rhymes and you'll be on your way to appreciating the Shakespearesque skill the poet employs here. And, having mentioned the bard, one way of thinking of the Duke is as kin to Shakespeare's duplicitous villains, Iago and Claudius might spring to mind. To appreciate Browning's technical accomplishment how about writing a reply to his poem in the form of a dramatic monologue in the voice of either the Count, the Duchess or the messenger?

Never stoop

The Duke is holding court. The eloquence of his words expresses his refined aristocratic manner. A domineering character, it seems he has total control of the narrative, speaking uninterrupted for 28 couplets. From the outset, he is in command, talking at, not with, the Count's messenger, politely condescending to him. Look, for example, at how he controls the topic of conversation, or how when he asks questions he doesn't wait for or allow a reply. Showing off his house and its possessions to indicate his power, prestige and wealth, the Duke establishes his credentials as a potential husband for the Count's daughter. The references to the artists, Fra Pandolf and Claus of Innsbruck, establish his cultural credentials, but also subtly contribute to the power-play. We do not know these artists and hence we are made to feel ignorant and inferior to the knowledgeable Duke. Extraordinarily self-assured, he high-handedly assumes that we, the listening audience, agree with his opinions. He portrays himself as a connoisseur of the arts and of good breeding. Indicating that he does not tolerate those who displease him, inadvertently, however, he reveals other, much darker aspects of his character. In this crucial way, Browning exerts control over the Duke.

We learn key things about the Duke's character:

- He is obsessed with control and possession
- He is extremely proud of his family heritage 'a nine-hundred years-old name'
- He has an exacting, refined sense of good taste 'here you miss / Or there you exceed the mark'
- He is breath-takingly arrogant, 'and I choose/never to stoop' (i.e. lower himself to explain how the Duchess's behaviour offended his sensibilities and pride)
- Crucially we also learn that he was murderously possessive and pathologically jealous: 'Since none puts by/ the curtain I have drawn for you, but I'.

Evil can come dressed in fine clothes, hidden by handsome manners. Slowly we come to realise that the accomplished, authoritative, intimidating manner of the Duke hides a monstrous nature: In truth, the Duke is a cruel, vindictive, merciless man. His perverse value system raises etiquette and social snobbery above morality. Specifically, he is a man who has had his wife murdered because she was too innocent, too friendly and kind-hearted: 'I gave commands/ Then all smiles stopped together'. And now he is turning his

 attention to a new potential wife who he refers to chillingly as his 'object'.

One of the most horrific aspects of the Duke's aristocratic hauteur is his refusal even to tell his dead wife how her actions so offended him. He denies her even the chance to amend her ways and so avoid her doom. He doesn't even tell her what he condemns her to death for. This is made even worse, if possible, by the fact that he refuses to inform her of what 'disgusts' him, simply because he regards this as beneath his dignity, 'I choose/ never to stoop'. It is chilling too how the Duke shows no remorse. And there is also no suggestion that he will, or could, be brought to justice for murder. Because he is a Duke he seems to be above and beyond the law. He could do with his wife as he liked because of who he was and the warped values of the society in which he lived.

The cultured impression we form of the Duke is generated by the language he uses and how he uses it. In addition to using complex vocabulary what is most striking is the Duke's syntax and sentence construction. Scan the poem quickly and you'll notice there are lots of hyphens, question marks and semi-colons. In themselves, these punctuation marks suggest linguistic complexity and this is enhanced by the construction of the Duke's sentences. The longest run over nine lines, moving forward, but also halting frequently, with many clauses and parentheses, giving the impression that the fastidious Duke is trying to be very precise and exact about what he is saying. There's something sinuous to how these long sentences uncoil across lines. In stark contrast the key lines in the poem are much shorter and blunter: 'This grew; I gave commands/ Then all smiles stopped together'.

The Duke's linguistic command is also conveyed metrically. In Renaissance literature, nobility of language is often taken to express nobility of character. A regular rhythm conveys poise and control over language. Here the language moves easily and fluently forward with the character speaking the lines fully in charge of what he is saying. Here is refined and elegant articulacy. A regular pattern also gives the poet something from which to deviate. In these deviations lies significance.

Look at the section from line 29 – 43, for instance, and you will see that the pattern of the verse becomes a little less smooth and regular. Browning achieves this by extensive use of caesura and hyphens. Line 31, for instance, contains multiple pauses, small hesitations and breaks in the flow: two beats then a comma, two more, then a full stop, three more beats followed by a comma and a hyphen, one beat and an exclamation mark. The disruption is enhanced by syntax that is contorted: The clause 'I know not how' is awkwardly stuck in the middle of the sentence and the exclamatory 'good' is suddenly interjected:

'...Or blush, at least. She thanked men, - good! but thanked...'

Despite the best efforts of our will, our body language often gives away what we are really feeling. Similarly, slips in the metrical pattern betray the Duke's uncharacteristic discomposure here, the difficulty he is having maintaining his facade. Simultaneously such metrical irregularities bring these crucial lines to our closer attention.

A heart too soon made glad

Her husband describes her in a way intended to make the listener unsympathetic to the Duchess. From the Duke's haughty point of view, she was far too free with her favour, just too friendly. But these qualities viewed

negatively by the Duke may well be read as positive attributes, especially by modern readers. For example, the Duchess is shown to have an intense emotional quality: 'the depth and passion' of an 'earnest glance', and a ready capacity for happiness, 'twas not/ her husband's presence only, called that spot/ of joy into the Duchess' cheek', she had a 'heart...too soon made glad'. She seems generous spirited, tending to 'like whate'er/ she looked on' and she is appreciative and courteous, 'she thanked men'. Whereas the Duke condemns her lack of discernment; the reader warms to her lack of snobbery and prejudice, her appreciation of simple, ordinary things: 'the dropping of the daylight...the white mule...all and each/ would draw from her alike the approving speech'. The Duke suggests that there may have been something flirtatious in her manner: 'her looks went everywhere'; we infer this perception is infected by his acute jealousy. 'Her looks went everywhere' may mean simple that she smiled at everyone.

What the Duke really cannot bear is her lack of appreciation for his aristocratic lineage: She seemed to weigh 'my gift of a nine-hundred-years-old name/ with anybody's gift'. In other words, she was not socially snobbish and did not behave as if she was superior to other people. To the Duke this behavior was an unforgivable insult to his pride and honour. So, we can conclude that the

Duke is haughty, emotionally and morally cold, as well as being supremely arrogant; the Duchess is his opposite; warm, vivacious, appreciative, charming. And for that he has her killed.

The painting of the Duchess is particularly significant. It reveals qualities of the central characters: the vivacity of the Duchess and the contrasting cold psychotic jealousy of her husband. Why is the Duke happier with the copy of the Duchess than with the real thing? Because he can control access to the painting, and because in it the Duchess is static, passive, unchanging. He views the painting and the person as possessions, the former adds to his status and esteem; alive, the Duchess detracted from it. A crucial detail is that 'Her mantle laps/ over my lady's wrist too much'. Like costumes in the theatre, dress in Renaissance paintings is very important. The mantle is the sleeve of her costume and it is a crucial, but characteristically ambiguous symbol. It suggests that there was something about the Duchess that was transgressive, 'laps over', and perhaps excessive 'too much'. In other words, in her own small way the Duchess stepped over boundaries. Of course, this quality can be viewed positively, reflecting somebody not bound by snobbish rules and regulations, someone who does not follow convention for convention's sake. But it can also be read negatively, as revealing someone who is ill mannered, who doesn't follow the correct polite behaviour. Moreover, it implies than even the very slightest non-compliance with strict rules, exceeding in some way 'the mark', will not only be noticed and frowned upon, but also severely punished.

The voice of Browning

As we have noted, the critical device used in dramatic monologues is irony. Irony undermines and transforms superficial meaning. And it is in the irony we hear the moral voice of the poet and his criticism of the values of society. Through picking up implied meaning, by reading between the lines, we hear Browning's voice behind the Duke's. For the Duke, addressing the messenger, his subject is his possessions, his house and especially his artworks. But, for Browning, addressing us, the readers, the subject is the Duke himself. The irony works against the Duke and in favour of the Duchess: The Duke presents himself in a way he assumes to be favourable. He assumes we will agree with his worldview, his values and his behaviour. He assumes will be impressed by his grand demeanour and style. In fact, his behaviour and his values are shown to be vile and reprehensible. What he takes to be taste, we read as snobbery; what he takes to be honour, we read as selfish egotism and pride; what he presents as good breeding, we read as cold, pathological, murderous jealousy.

A noble frame

Browning's poem is one long, solid and unbroken stanza, comprising 28 rhymed couplets. If it were a building the poem would be a palace, or perhaps an elegant and well-constructed fortress. There are no breaks, or gaps or chinks of weakness in this fortress. The form of rhymed iambic couplets Browning employs is sometimes called heroic verse, a form that constitutes another part of the façade of the Duke. The elegant, noble form of heroic verse, clicking harmoniously into its repeated patterns is like expensive clothes and fine manners, hiding the fundamental monstrosity of the Duke. The poise and balance of the verse is his outer manner in action. Moreover, as Stephen Fry writes, Browning creates a 'ironic contrast between the urbane conversational manner, the psychotic darkness of the story and the elegant solidity of a noble form. The heroic verse is the frame out of which character can leap; it is itself the nobly proportioned, exquisitely tasteful palace in which ignobly misproportioned, foully tasteless deeds are done'. [3]

My Last Duchess crunched:

Duchess – alive – wonder – stands – look – design – strangers – earnest – none – I – seemed – how – sir – husband's – joy – laps –

---
[3] *The Ode Less Travelled*, p.206

too – faint – dies – thought – joy – heart – easily – everywhere – my – dropping – fool – mule – all – approving – thanked – ranked – gift – anybody's – trifling – will – just – disgusts – exceed – lessoned – excuse – stooping – never – without – commands – stopped – alive – repeat – master's – pretense – dowry – daughter's – object – Neptune – taming – me.

NB

Despite the hostility of her domineering father, in 1846 Robert Browning secretly courted and married Elizabeth Barrett. A few days later the two poets escaped family and society outrage by eloping to Italy. Their shocking behaviour was condemned stridently by Elizabeth's father, who disinherited her, and by her brothers. Six years older than Robert, Elizabeth had been a recluse and was disabled; hence she did fit the convention of the perfect wife. Though Browning's poem features Renaissance characters, it is simultaneously about Victorian society and powerfully expresses a growing awareness of, and protest against, the abuse of women by patriarchal society.

Alfred Lord Tennyson, *The Charge of the Light Brigade*

Us vs. them

For a poem so stuffed with soldiers and horses and cannons, there is a rather faceless quality to the entire affair. Tennyson creates the sterile stereotypes that are necessary in all conflicts: Us and Them. The doomed brilliance of the British army is captured by the 'noble six hundred', who seem to act as one entity.

The British soldiers embody the type of bravery that resulted in the largest empire since ancient Rome. Not only are they courageous and 'noble' but they are unquestioning too: 'Theirs not to reason why.' We must remember that in Tennyson's day, such unquestioning obedience was to be praised. After the twentieth century's world wars and Vietnam, and with changing conceptions of the afterlife, such automatic and unquestioning obedience may be seen as foolish nowadays.

The Light Brigade epitomize speed, action and courage. Even their physical position, on horseback, elevates them symbolically above their enemies. They are also associated with light in terms of God and goodness, with Tennyson here playing on their military classification. Such positive connotations are continued in the use of the verb 'flashed' as the Light Brigade engage with the opposition. This association with light is slyly associated with right as they beam through the gloom of the 'battery-smoke'.

Waiting for them at the other end of the 'valley of Death' lie the enemy: the Russians and Cossacks. In contrast to the dynamic movement of the Light Brigade, they simply sit and wait, plotting the downfall of their noble adversaries.  Even their weapon of choice tells us something of their dubious personalities: cannons versus sabres. Surely no contest? Unfortunately, for them their smugness is about to be 'shattered and sundered by the rapid romantic sabres of the Light Brigade. The important verb 'reeled' suggests enemy weakness in the face of overwhelming valour, despite the disastrous reality of the situation. This discrepancy between the two fighting groups magnifies the feats of the Light Brigade whilst simultaneously belittling the fighting prowess of the Russians. Tennyson seems to be saying 'Go Britannia'! even when the British are going in the wrong direction to almost certain death!

There is also another group which we must consider; a group who are responsible for the event, but not for the bravery. The commands of Lord Raglan create the opportunity for British fighting men to shine when confronted by high danger. However, how should we respond to the crucial verb 'blundered'? We are now firmly located in that age-old wartime debate about who commands and who fights and, more importantly, who gets the glory of martial success. Such debates stretch back as far as Homer's *Iliad*, where Achilles gets put out by his commander's (Agamemnon) demands for the spoils of war. We remember Nelson and Churchill, but who were the brave souls who actually did the fighting? And that is partly the problem. For a more modern take on this tension between commanders and commanded, we need to look forward to the poetry of Siegfried Sassoon and Wilfred Owen.

Let there be (no) blood

You don't need a Degree in English Literature to recognize the dominance of war imagery in the poem, but what is striking is the distinct lack of violence. *Saving Private Ryan* it is not! This is poetry written in an age preoccupied with moral decency and glory; blood splattered poetry would horrify rather than rouse Tennyson's reading public. Tennyson instead creates a very dramatic, almost cinematic, poem that focuses on movement. The driving force of the Brigade itself hurtles the reader into the midst of the battle, where Tennyson surrounds us with the sounds of war as opposed to the sights. A real sense of forward momentum is generated by:

- verbs like 'charge'
- the quasi-onomatopoeic 'plunged'
- the metre
- the short line lengths

The first image of note is one where Tennyson makes it clear that this is not just some propagandist vehicle hurrahing the might of the British Military. When he proclaims that the Light Brigade are charging across 'the valley of Death' we are left in no uncertain terms that destruction and loss is inevitable. In one way, of course, this makes the feat of the Light Brigade even more awe-inspiring (or stupid). The valley of Death delivers a clear biblical clang for Tennyson's Victorian audience as it borrows from Psalm 23: 'Yea, though I walk through the valley of the shadow of death, I will fear no evil: for thou art with me; thy rod and thy staff they comfort me'. This imaginatively captures the physical space of the battle i.e. a valley but also manages to foreshadow the massive losses suffered by the Light Brigade.

The valley of death becomes almost a motif that Tennyson uses throughout the poem, sometimes with interesting variations. The valley of death is repeated in stanza two and in stanza three is developed by linking death with hell itself. The valley of death becomes 'the jaws of death', which personifies death as an all- consuming monster. Tennyson cleverly links the 'jaws' to the 'mouth', but the mouth now belongs to hell rather than death itself. The gothic imagery suggests that the Light Brigade are food for the war machine. Again, this particular coupling of 'jaws of Death' and 'mouth of hell' appears in the fifth stanza. This time, though, the Light Brigade retreat back rather than charge into the terrible site of violence.

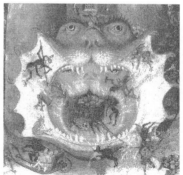

Auditory imagery, associated with the cannons that pepper the charging cavalry, is particularly powerful. The fact that cannons lined both sides of the valley, as well as awaited them at the valley's end, meant that the Light Brigade were showered with deadly explosives from all angles. The booming cannons are captured through:

- The mere repetition of the word itself. The repetition of 'cannon' at the start of stanza three mimics the sequential firing of the cannons.
- Repetition is employed again in the fifth stanza where the Light Brigade must face the firing cannons for the second time.
- Tennyson employs storm imagery to capture the reality of the battlefield where he uses the verb 'thundered'. This evokes not only the sound of the cannons but also strengthens the foreshadowing that all hell is about to break loose.
- Tennyson stretches this imagery by using another related verb: 'stormed': The 'shot and shell' from the cannons rains down on them in a storm of fire.

This fourth stanza also contains possibly the most important visual image in the poem: that of the Light Brigade's bright sabres. Another example of repetition, the key word in the opening couplet is 'Flashed'. The brightness of the metal sabres carries a positivity that contrasts with the dark cannons. It also intensifies the drama of Tennyson's cinematic treatment - the gleaming blades slicing through the oppressive enemy smoke. By using the hand held light sabres it elevates the British soldiers above their enemies.

This is interesting imagery itself: These verbs don't seem to suit actions suffered by humans, but rather damage made to a faceless machine. Again, it is more difficult to sympathise with enemy robots being dismantled than seeing fellow human beings brutally sliced and diced in your name.

A strategy of repetition

As in many poems, repetition is a key device in *The Charge of the Light Brigade*. The first example of the strategy of repetition is at the very start: 'Half a league, half a league, / Half a league onward'. The caesura right in the middle of the opening line creates a sense of balance before the onward thrust of the second line. Repetition of 'half a league' also allows the narrator to present the point of view of the cavalrymen. There is no doubt as to whose side we are to be on. It also creates suspense; the moment of engagement must be waited for, by both Light Brigade and reader. The first line also mimics the galloping of the charging horses in its sound effects (try it yourself and see what rhythm you construct). This metre never relents, which further adds to the poem's forward momentum.

Tennyson also uses what might be termed a refrain, or a repeated section, at the end of each stanza. Again, to avoid exhaustion of effect he wisely introduces variation. Looking at the following excerpts we can see this refrain in action:

> 'Into the valley of Death / Rode the six Hundred'
> 'Into the valley of Death / Rode the six Hundred'
> 'Into the mouth of hell / Rode the six Hundred'
> 'Then they rode back, but not / Not the six Hundred'
> 'All that was left of them / Left of six Hundred'
> Noble six hundred!'

While obviously the changes reflect the movement of the Light Brigade into and out of the battle, the inescapable entity is the Light Brigade itself. Note the clever use of caesura and word repetition as they charge back. Look at the dramatic pause after 'Then they rode back', which allows the reader a brief moment of contemplation, which is then coloured with sadness by the repetition of 'not'. Ditto for the repetition of 'left'; it is simple, but devastating. Tennyson concentrates on the collective, the six hundred, rather than any individual, which would have amplified the potential for sympathy from the reader. At the end of the poem it is impossible to forget the six hundred and not only that but due to his clever variations, what lingers is the last trumpeting line, celebrating the nobility of these fighting men.

Of all the repeated phrases used by Tennyson surely it is the 'Honour…Honour' couplet in the final stanza that is most important. This drives home the expected emotional response for the reader and it is hard to argue with the events as described in the poem. The other significant example is Tennyson's condensation of the soldier's duty on the battlefield: 'Theirs not to make reply / Theirs not to reason why / Theirs but to do and die.' Whilst espousing the bravery of the men themselves for Tennyson's Victorian audience, it also leaves itself open to exploitation in the name of propaganda. Again, the First World War and the senseless losses suffered on both sides springs to a modern mind.

Order vs. chaos

The first thing notable about Tennyson's form is its irregularity: Six stanzas of varying lengths: eight lines, nine lines, nine lines, 12 lines, 11 lines and finally six lines. Such irregularity is unusual in Victorian poetry. The rhyming scheme adds to the tension between regularity and irregularity. It is clearly irregular, as it varies from stanza to stanza, but the reoccurrence of certain units in the stanzas lends familiarity and maybe the illusion of regularity. Visually the individual rhyme schemes look like this:

ABCBDDCB
AABCDDDEC
AAABCCDCB
AAABCDDEDCFC
AAABCCCDCEB
AABAAB.

There is clearly variation in each stanza. Not one has the same rhyme scheme but the occurrence of couplets and triplets is common. A strong connection between all the stanzas is Tennyson's imperfect rhyme with the word 'hundred'. He uses 'blundered', 'thundered' and 'wondered' towards the beginning of each stanza with the 'hundred' always the last word in the stanza. Obviously, Tennyson repeatedly brings the attention of the reader to the 'six hundred', but the three rhyme words can be seen to encapsulate the entire poem: the miscommunication, the peril, the glory.

Constant pulling between regularity and irregularity creates a somewhat destabilized feel which mirrors the descent into chaos that confronts the Light Brigade. It also could link to the chaos of war trying to be controlled by military organization. The emphasis on planning and strategy in military operations is key but can be undone simply by the pure haphazard nature of conflict itself.

Of course, Tennyson's use of metre is crucial. He chooses a rare form: the amphimaceric tetrameter. While sounding like a small yet vital gauge in an airplane cockpit, it simply means that Tennyson predominantly uses three syllable combinations that sound like tum-ti-tum. Of course, there's no need for you to use such technical language for GCSE. The crucial thing is to notice that the metre mimics the sound of the thundering, charging horses.

The structure of the poem is almost narrative driven. Again, the structure is not symmetrical but yet there is a clear reflection, albeit a distorted one. We see the charge into enemy lines mirrored by the retreat back, but there is also the treatment of the fatal blunder in stanza two, which technically should start the poem. Tennyson instead chooses to start the poem in media res, as they are charging. This creates a real sense of excitement at the start instead, which may not have been achievable if sticking to a strictly chronological structure. He does get the end of the poem spot on as it builds to a suitably celebratory climax.

Balaclava

The Charge of the Light Brigade was a charge of British cavalry led by Lord Cardigan against Russian forces during the Battle of Balaclava on 25 October

LORD RAGLAN.

1854 in the Crimean War. Lord Raglan, overall commander, intended to send the Light Brigade to pursue and harry a retreating Russian artillery battery near the front line, a task well suited to light cavalry. Due to miscommunication at some level in the chain of command, the sabre-armed Light Brigade was instead sent on a frontal assault into a different artillery battery, one well-prepared with excellent fields of defensive fire. Although reaching the battery under withering direct fire and scattering some of the gunners, the badly mauled brigade was forced to retreat immediately, producing no decisive gains and very high British casualties. Blame for the miscommunication has remained controversial, as the original order from Raglan itself was vague. Tennyson read about it in The Times and wrote the poem minutes later.

The Charge crunched:

League – onward – death – rode – forward – valley – six hundred – light brigade – dismayed – soldier – blundered – theirs – reason – die – valley – six hundred – cannon – left – front – thundered – stormed – boldly – jaws – mouth – six hundred – sabres – flashed – gunners – army – wondered – plunged – broke – cossack – reeled – shattered – cannon – left – behind – volleyed – shell – hero – fought – death – hell – left of

them - six hundred – glory – wild – wondered – honour – light brigade – noble.

Wilfred Owen, *Exposure*

We cringe in holes

As we have just seen, Tennyson's adrenalin-fuelled poem is packed-to-the-gills with vigorous, dynamic action. The poem sets off at a terrific rhythmical lick and the galloping pace does not let up until it reaches its heroic climax. Despite celebrating a defeat, Tennyson's poem is a boys' own adventure story version of war, full of flashing sabres, canon fire, pounding and thudding of horses' hooves. *The Charge of the Light Brigade* is heroic, dynamic, explosive and, moreover, exciting; there's no sense of suffering, or bloodshed or pain in this manly pseudo-sport. Owen's poem, of course, could not be more different. Indeed, it could be read as a corrective to Tennyson's patriotic and romanticised version of warfare. If Tennyson's poem is characterised by action, inaction is the key aspect of Owen's poem. It was passive inaction that particularly shredded the nerves of soldiers fighting in the trenches of WWI. Most of the time soldiers stuck in trenches simply had to endure; waiting helplessly, coping with the boredom and the atrocious conditions - the rats, the lice, the mud, the cold, the endless pounding of artillery - and then death could just come suddenly, seemingly randomly, as a shell exploded or, as in Owen's poem, the weather conditions lulled you to death. There was little you could do to prepare or protect yourself, or your comrades. The mood and atmosphere in Owen's poem is of lingering, impotent dread.

Whereas Tennyson's poem clearly delineates the goodies (us noble Brits) from the baddies (those darned Ruskies), Owen's does not distinguish German from Brits. Despite the virulent wartime propaganda about the monstrous 'Hun', there is no sense in Owen's poem that the Germans are the enemy. The weather, the generals who have left their men in these conditions, the callous people at home, even God is a possible enemy in *Exposure*. Germans though aren't even mentioned. Indeed the soldiers depicted could be German; their nationality is immaterial to Owen. His poem is concerned with pity and compassion for humanity.

Bullets...less deathly than the air

Owen's opening phase 'Our brains ache' mirrors the opening to the Romantic poet, John Keats' *Ode to a Nightingale*: 'My heart aches', suggesting from the start a strong connection to one of Owen's most admired poets and the ideas Keats expressed within his poetry. Alongside exploration of the darker side of humanity and the pain and suffering endured as part of human existence, nature is a major theme throughout the Romantic movement, as touched upon elsewhere within this guide. Predominantly nature is depicted as a source of beauty, understanding and inspiration by the Romantic poets. Dawn and spring were common motifs, often symbolising new beginnings, new hope and the warm benevolence of nature. In stark contrast in Owen's poem the dawn is presented as an enemy. This is just one of the ways in which in *Exposure* the poet highlights the mortal threat posed by nature, and the irony that despite living in a war zone, the 'bullets' are 'less deathly than the air'.

The exposed conditions of the trenches in world war one are brutally portrayed throughout, with repeated images of the 'merciless iced wind', which 'knive' the men in stanza one; the dawn 'massing' a 'melancholy army' which 'attacks once more' in stanza three, until finally in the last stanza the 'frost will fasten on this mud and us' and in a particularly chilling, almost Gothic image 'all their eyes are ice'. The cruel irony is reinforced through the

juxtaposition of the potency the personified weather has, to inflict pain and suffering, with the total lack of agency contained within any images of the military efforts. 'Low, drooping flares', the 'dull rumour' of the 'flickering gunnery', and the bullets that are 'less deathly than the air' create a sense of impotence around the war effort. The verb 'drooping', especially, has a bitter, mocking tone, demonstrating the feeling that nothing is achieved by their presence here.

But nothing happens

It is important to understand just how incongruous Owen's message within his poetry was; the British prided themselves in keeping a 'stiff upper lip', and he was strongly criticised for what many felt were unpatriotic sentiments. 'Passive suffering is not a theme for poetry', wrote the famous poet Yeats, an attitude echoed by many who felt that the soldiers should tolerate these horrific conditions without question. Think, for instance, of Tennyson's lines, 'theirs not to reason why/ theirs but to do and die'.

Owen not only highlights the suffering endured by the soldiers during the endless months in the trenches, but also repeatedly comes back to the impotence of the war effort. 'My theme is war and the pity of war' he stated elsewhere, and there is nothing more harrowing than the 'pity' of these men losing their lives while all the while 'nothing happens'; a phrase repeated at the end of four of the eight stanzas. The use of the refrain itself suggests a lack of development; we move on but return to the same phrase. It also implies that the men are losing their lives for 'nothing', for no gain or purpose. The title of the poem 'Exposure' not only relates to the threat of death by this means, but also the fact that Owen is 'exposing' the reality of war and the lack of care for these men. War, in Owen's poem, is not the honourable and glorious battle in which men fight for their lives and die with courage and bravery: far from it. They lie night after night in the freezing cold until 'all their eyes are ice...but nothing happens'. This final line is a sickening twist which hammers home the futility of, rather than the honour in, their deaths.

Slowly our ghosts drag home...

Alongside the repeated images of impotent weaponry and inaction, Owen further builds the sense of interminable misery through the irregular, almost laboured rhythm and rhyme scheme. The first four lines of each stanza are typically hexameter (six metrical 'feet' of two syllables), but Owen adds additional syllables or feet to some lines, seemingly without any set pattern. The final line of each stanza is much shorter and blunter and varies in length, causing the pace to slow almost to a stop again and again as the stanzas creep forward. Compare these long, stretched out lines with the short, dynamic ones used by Tennyson and you'll notice the way they slow the poem down to almost to a standstill. The metrical pulse too is very muted, like a faint and inconstant heartbeat.

The rigid overarching structure of eight stanzas with four longer lines and one shorter one could indicate that on a surface level there is organisation and clarity; it is only when you attempt to read the poem and are halted by the stumbling rhythm that you realise this was an illusion. Perhaps this could mirror the manner in which the war effort to those on the outside may appear coordinated and well assembled; it is only when you are on the inside experiencing it that you understand how directionless and disjointed it really is. Another way of thinking of the form is in terms of repetition: Eight stanzas following the same slow, drawn out, unchanging pattern evoke a sense of stasis or, perhaps, suspended animation.

Pararhyme - partial or imperfect rhyme which does not rhyme fully but uses similar vowel sounds - is used to create a sense of dissonance in the rhyme scheme. Half rhymes are often placed between similar sounding consonants, for example 'knife us' / 'nervous', 'silent' / 'salient', 'Wire/war'. This makes for a jarring read; rather than being allowed to gain the satisfaction of a complete and 'fitting' rhyme, instead we are left with something imperfect and discordant, reinforcing the sense of stasis created by the halting rhythm and the refrain, 'nothing happens'.

Love of God seems dying

The eventual deaths of the men at the end of the poem is mirrored by the apparent death of their faith in stanza seven; once again a highly controversial notion for Owen to put forward to a British society with a churchgoing populace. More disturbing than the idea that the men are losing their love of God however, is the suggestion that God maybe losing his love of them. Worse still, the personification of the weather from the start of the poem takes a sinister tone towards the end when 'our love is made afraid' of 'God's invincible spring'. Like nature, God is presented here not just as potentially indifferent to the men's suffering, but as an active enemy of man. The idea is reinforced in the final stanza when 'His frost will fasten on this mud and us', as if God is in control of the weather and is 'merciless' in his 'Shrivelling' of 'many hands', and 'puckering' of 'foreheads crisp'. The disgust created in this image is reinforced by the aural image; the sound of the almost onomatopoeic 'crisp' forces the reader to imagine human flesh crinkling as it turns to ice.

Indeed, this is a very tactile poem. Owen gets as close as he can to making us feel the physical sensations the soldiers endure. This is particularly disturbing when the poet combines touch with images that elsewhere would suggest intimacy and love. Look, for instance, at the alliterative line, 'Pale flakes with fingering stealth come feeling for our faces'. This is death, creeping up on the soldier as a kind of perverse, tempting lover, a lover that will gently touch their faces and lull them into a drowsy 'snow-daze', a dreamy numbness that could prove fatal.

Harsh consonant sounds add to the sense of bitterness which pervades the poem, and once the reader reaches the end we understand that this bitterness is not just directed towards the officialdom of the British army, but also towards God. The early 'merciless iced east winds which knive us' contains the hard consonants 'c' and 't' which create a cutting tone, combined with the sibilant repeated 's's which mimic the sound of this biting wind and recreate its coldness. This continues in stanza three with 'lasts', 'soaks', 'clouds sag stormy', 'massing', 'east', 'attacks', 'ranks' and 'shivering' and in stanza four where 'Sudden successive flights of bullets streak the silence' and the air 'shudders' with 'snow'. The bitterness is also directed towards those at home who the soldiers no longer are able to make a connection with. The soldiers' 'ghosts' drag home where they realise that the 'Shutters and doors all closed'; a combination of harsh consonant and sibilance sounds in this image creating a sense of finality associated with resentment as they 'turn back to [their] dying'. This moment is perhaps the most disturbing of all: Despite the horror and dread and creeping death, the men make the conscious decision to return to the trenches and endure the futile death expected of them.

Exposure crunched:

Merciless – night – confuse – nervous – nothing – mad – agonies – gunnery – war – what – misery – lasts – melancholy – attacks – nothing – bullets – deadly – flashes – wind's – nothing – stealth – holes – sun-dozed – blossoms – dying – ghosts - dark-red – innocent – closed – dying – believe – smile – God's – lie – dying – frost – shrivelling – shaking – ice – nothing.

Ted Hughes, *Bayonet Charge*

Inspired by the great war poets such as Wilfred Owen, and by the stories of his father's exploits in World War One, Hughes' poem examines the experience of an individual soldier on the battlefield. Moving away from the idea of collective identity and soldiery seen in poems such as *The Charge of the Light Brigade*, Hughes explores the thoughts and feelings of a single soldier as he struggles towards enemy lines. The enemy is not known; neither is the allegiance of the soldier himself, though we might assume he is British due to the possible mention of George V in 'King'. It is the individual soldier's experience that is the focus of this poem - a universal experience. We see the fighting through the febrile eyes of an anonymous soldier, the focus on conflict (both external and internal) rather than country.

Suddenly he awoke

Beginning *in media res*, *Bayonet Charge* opens with no explanation of what is happening. Like the soldier, we are thrown into a state of confusion. No immediate reason is given as to why the soldier is 'running' – indeed, we are not even explicitly told that the 'he' mentioned is a soldier. Although we are given small details throughout the poem, we are never allowed to know the setting or context as a whole; we remain as disorientated as the soldier is throughout.

The nightmarish opening of 'Suddenly he awoke and was running' bears witness to a soldier 'suddenly' realising the reality and urgency of his situation, the dramatic adverb highlighting his panic. Awaking from the patriotic dream of 'King, honour, human dignity', the soldier is utterly unprepared for the realities of warfare; he runs 'raw - /In raw-seamed hot khaki'. Repetition here emphasises his discomfort – discomfort with his ill-fitting uniform, but also with his role in the conflict. Recalling the phrase 'raw recruits', 'raw' also highlights inexperience and youth, and recalls images of raw meat and cows sent to slaughter. This soldier is not charging boldly towards death; he is terrified, alone, bewildered.

The first stanza showcases the brutal intrusion of reality as the nameless soldier realises the danger he is in. He is overwhelmed by exhaustion and terror. The physical and emotional strain is made clear as he wears his 'hot khaki, his sweat heavy'. The headlong rush of that eleven-line long, breathless first sentence, with its repetitive vocabulary, density of present participle verbs and loose construction, evokes heavy breathing as the soldiers runs and we are never fully certain whether he is panting from exertion or terror. The repeated references to 'sweat' pose a similar dilemma – is the soldier sweating because he is physically drained, or because he is consumed by his terror? Regardless, he is clearly losing control of both the situation and his body. Verbs such as 'stumbling' suggest lack of control over his actions; indeed, the entire line 'stumbling across a field of clods towards a green hedge' creates a choppy, uncertain rhythm, reflecting the soldier's struggle navigating the landscape. He is physically exhausted: his gun is not carried, but 'lugged'. He is disorientated, so 'dazzled' by the rifle fire of enemy lines that he fixes on an inanimate object rather than a specific enemy. His gun is 'numb as a smashed arm', perhaps reflecting his own body shutting down. He, like the gun, feels broken and useless.

Clearly the gun foreshadows the injuries the soldier may suffer and it supports the violent imagery already present in the plosive 'bullets smacking the belly out of the air'. Yet it also symbolises how the soldier has become numb to the reasons why he signed up to fight in the war in the first place. It is interesting that the simile is linked by a semi-colon to the description of 'the patriotic tear that had brimmed in his eye /Sweating like molten iron from the centre of his chest'. The soldier's gun is useless because he is no longer sure what he is fighting for. Patriotism has been shoved aside by a painful reality. It is this, more than the battle itself, that disorientates the soldier. Without his patriotic ideals, the world seems to have turned inside out. A 'smashed arm' is a brutal image that we associate with agony, not numbness; the image of 'bullets smacking the belly out of the air' is similarly inverted. Rather than an image of air being punched out of someone, as we expect when someone is winded, here the 'belly' is being punched out of the air itself. Everything that made sense to the soldier has become lost in the haze of battle. He is like a lost, confused child, echoed in the oddly childlike punishment of 'smacking'.

As the poem progresses, we see the soldier lose progressively more of his individuality until he transforms from a thinking human being into a dangerous

weapon. Consumed by fear, he becomes little more than an animal. Like the hare that crawls, 'its mouth wide / Open silent, its eyes standing out', he is unable to express agony and terror. He is voiceless, unable to change his fate – he is, just like the hare, prey. The bathos of 'King, honour, human dignity,' and the tellingly dismissive 'etcetera' clearly shows how futile this ideology is in war; the anticlimactic ending suggesting that the reasons for going to war are no longer even worth mentioning. The soldier attacks out of a desperate desire to survive, not moral principle. In reality, these ideas are mere 'luxuries'; the soldier is reduced to a state of animalistic fear, only able to express himself through a meaningless, unreasoned 'yelling alarm'. By the end of the poem, his nerves are stretched to their limit and he is lost to his explosive fear. We are left with the final metaphor of 'his terror's touchy dynamite', an alliterative image that suggests he is ready to explode at the slightest touch. War has destroyed his patriotic ideals; all that is left is destruction and fear.

He almost stopped

Notably, *Bayonet Charge* does not follow a rhyme scheme or any sort of formal structure. The experience of the soldier is expressed instead through sentence construction, line length, enjambment and pacing. The first stanza showcases the strain the soldier is under, long vowels stretching words and slowing the pace at times to mimic his unsteady progression across the field. The third stanza passes by in a blur of hurtling terror as the soldier loses the capacity for higher reasoning. Yet it is the second, with its long, drawn out contemplation, that is the most interesting.

Contrasting heavily with the first and third stanzas, the poem's middle section is dedicated not to the external, physical conflict the soldier is engaged in, but to the internal one inside his head. A stolen moment of introspection on the battlefield, an entire stanza occurs within the time given it takes to make a single step. Here, we do not see the increasing panic and confusion of the other stanzas; instead, we witness a rational, intelligent man wondering how he got to this terrifying point in his life.

The 'patriotic tear that had brimmed in his eye' gone forever. The soldier is lost in 'bewilderment'. His unthinking obedience to the army falters as, mid-charge, he starts to wonder why he is there. The dash at the end of 'he almost stopped' abruptly shortens the line, pausing the action and creating a sudden stillness that takes the reader out of the conflict and into the soldier's head. Although the stanza still primarily focuses on fear, lingering on the image of 'a man who has jumped up in the dark' and fled from his nightmares, there is a sense of distance here, of emotional detachment. Whilst the quick pace created through enjambment and the repetition of 'running' hurries the stanza along, we do not feel any of the panic or confusion of the previous stanza. Indeed, the juxtaposition between the running man and the calmness of the soldier is only emphasised by the simile 'his foot hung like /Statuary in mid stride'; the sense of immobility reinforced through the following caesura. Sandwiched between the two images of frozen movement, the running man becomes something more than a simplistic idea of fear – he becomes a symbol of the futility of the war.

Running 'in the dark' and listening 'for the reason /Of his still running', the man in this stanza is presented as being both blind and irrational. Unable to see where he is going, or why he is even running, he represents the soldier's sudden realisation of the pointlessness of war. The soldier no longer feels he is fighting for any good reason – he is isolated, alone, part of the bigger picture, but unable to relate to it. When he asks himself 'in what cold clockwork of the stars and the nations /Was he the hand pointing that second?', the soldier has suddenly, fully realised his insignificance. Whilst he is the 'hand' of conflict, a synecdoche for the nation he represents, he is still the 'second' hand; a small, near-meaningless measurement of time. In comparison to the larger units of 'nations' and space, he is irrelevant, miniscule. Like the ticking of the clock, war is inevitable – it does not matter if he is there or not. It will continue regardless. The harsh 'c' and 'k' consonance of 'cold clockwork' emphasises his isolation. He is, he realises, unimportant and his own nation does not care about him.

The green hedge

Between the vivid, onomatopoeic depiction of physical conflict in stanzas one and three, and the internal conflict portrayed in stanza two, it is perhaps easy to forget the third, hidden conflict within Hughes' poem. With the lack of a clearly identifiable enemy, at times it almost feels like the soldier and his allies are attacking Nature itself.

There is a clear message within this poem about the destructive nature of conflict. In the first stanza, the 'field of clods' the soldier runs over are juxtaposed with the 'green hedge' he runs towards. What was once a fertile field, capable of bearing crops has, due to human conflict, become nothing more than lumps of earth. As the soldier charges towards the unspoilt 'green hedge', blending the inanimate object with the enemy firing upon him in his confused state, there is a sense that Nature is under attack by humanity. The image that is strengthened in the final stanza, as the soldier 'plunged past with his bayonet toward the green hedge'. With no mention of an enemy force, it is the repeated imagery of the 'green hedge' that seems to become the soldier's adversary.

The 'shot-slashed furrows' that throw the soldier out of his introspection further reinforces the theme of Man versus Nature; alliterative and hard to say out loud without slowing the pace, it draws our attention to the contrast between growth and destruction. Whilst a farmer would plough the earth to grow crops and create life, here the earth has been changed through the armies' attempts to kill their enemies. Nature, it appears, is sick and dying. The hare is described as 'yellow' – whilst this could symbolise the soldier's own fear due to the typical association of the  colour with cowardice. But it also has connotations of sickness and life withering away. Rolling 'like a flame', the hare is in agony. The use of the agricultural term 'threshing' adds to the idea that Nature is devastated by war as the hare writhes in pain. Its helpless, crawling movements reflect the damage mankind is wreaking upon Nature; its terrified expression with 'its mouth wide /Open silent, its eyes standing out' show how vulnerable the hare is.

Human dignity, etcetera

Whilst we can assume that the poem centres on a soldier charging an enemy trench in World War One, Hughes' poem does not hinge on any particular single moment in time. His exploration of both the internal and external conflicts of war, alongside the examination of the effect war has on Nature, allows Hughes to explore the nature of conflict itself. The soldier's experience is a universal one, not tied to any specific battle, or even any particular country. Conflict, Hughes suggests, is both physically and mentally devastating, destroying our natural surroundings and our own sense of self. It is a cold, almost mechanical experience, as inevitable as the progression of time itself. The hare's 'threshing circle' is perhaps not just an expression of agony; it is also a commentary on the nature of conflict itself. Like a circle, it has no end and is pointless. Nothing is really gained. And so much is lost.

Bayonet Charge crunched:

Suddenly – awoke – raw – sweat – heavy – stumbling – clods – green - hedge – smacking – numb – smashed – patriotic – bewilderment – stopped – cold - running – dark – statuary – furrows – yellow – hare – crawled – threshing – circle – silent – honour – dignity – etcetera – luxuries – alarm – dynamite.

Seamus Heaney, *Storm on the Island*

One of the first poems published by Heaney, *Storm on the Island* appeared in *The New Statesman* in 1964 and is reflective both of his strong connection with nature and his homeland of Northern Ireland. With its depiction of a landscape hunkering down under a severe pummelling of winds, exploding seas and 'bombardments' of air, the poem explores the challenges posed to humans exposed to the wild forces of nature on the Aran Islands. Much has been written regarding this interpretation; Heaney himself has referred to the barren landscape of the Aran islands as offering him inspiration for the poem. Indeed, throughout his career, Heaney continued to celebrate characters and places which showed the fortitude to endure, to, in his words 'keep going', however tough life might become. And certainly, this is one way to read this poem. But, whilst there are many different interpretations of this poem, and what the 'storm' could represent on a more figurative level, this essay will develop a political reading, specifically the idea the island depicts in this poem stands in for the island of Ireland, and that the weather symbolises the turbulent nature of life as an inhabitant of Northern Island, in particular, during the centuries-old conflict between nationalist and loyalist forces.

Stormont

Heaney adopts the pronoun 'we' throughout the poem, as opposed to the first person 'I', as he has chosen to do in a number of poems throughout his collections. He has explained the key difference in this lexical choice, stating that these poems are not specifically autobiographical; for this he adopts the first-person pronoun 'I'. He uses 'we' in poetry which reflects wider cultural experiences, and the ongoing conflict endured in Northern Ireland could certainly be viewed as a collective experience.

To fully appreciate the context of this conflict, it is necessary to delve briefly into the history of the Northern Irish conflict, which has its origins as far back as the late 12th century when Britain invaded and took control of Ireland in its entirety. The British began small-scale immigration settling of the land, which the Irish resisted at every turn, with many uprisings against their imperialist oppressors. They remained in control however, and in the 16th century Britain increased the scale of its immigration, with huge areas of land confiscated from the Irish inhabitants to create large and profitable plantations. This had a greater impact on uprooting the culture and identity of the traditionally Catholic Irish, with the increasing number of ruling Protestant communities. This was particularly evident in the north or Ireland, where large numbers of predominantly Protestants from Scotland settled. The Irish managed to rise-up and overthrow the British during the 16th century, with the exception of a hard core of Scots Protestants in Northern Ireland. In 1922 the southern provinces of Ireland gained independence from Britain and became known as a separate country, with Northern Ireland remaining part of the UK.

Heaney was born in 1939 as a Catholic in Northern Ireland, at a time when Catholics were essentially the 'underclass' as they still lived under the rule of the Protestant government. They faced discrimination and persecution from the government and police, and although the civil rights movement, formed to fight for equal rights, did not gain its full momentum until after Heaney wrote *Storm on the Island*, there was a strong political and guerrilla warfare movement against the injustice levelled against the Irish Catholics which included the 'Border Campaign' between 1956 and 1962. This aimed to overthrow British rule and re-unite Ireland under Irish rule, and undoubtedly would have had a profound impact on Heaney who lived through the ongoing battle on his doorstep.

So, what evidence can we identify which supports the view that this 'storm' is a metaphorical representation of the military conflict in Northern Ireland? Let's start by looking at the title '**Storm on t**he Island'. The first eight letters spell out 'Stormont', the name of the building which, at the time Heaney wrote the poem, housed the Parliament of Northern Ireland. This was the political centre, arguably the 'epicentre' of the political 'storm' which had waged throughout the nation for centuries.

The extended metaphor of the 'Island' as a battleground is continued throughout the poem through the semantic field of warfare. The opening statement: 'We are prepared' feels like a challenge; the 'we' evoking the sense of a unified force ready to take whatever their common enemy throws at them. A colon introduces a list of preparations they have made to their defences, relayed in the present tense 'we build', 'sink walls' and 'roof...with good slate'. It is significant that Heaney only makes references to defence and protection; there is no sense that this is an enemy to be attacked in return; it must simply be withstood as they 'sit tight' and wait for it to pass. More dynamic, aggressive verbs are allocated to the enemy which 'blows full blast'; the repeated plosives here creating an aural image of the violence. It 'pummels your house' - the shift to the second person involving the reader in the drama, perhaps making them consider the extent to which they are also subjected to the force of this metaphorical enemy. The semantic field continues right to the end of the poem, through the present participle verbs, 'exploding' and 'strafes', placing the reader at the heart of the action, then finally the lexical choices of 'salvo', and 'bombarded'. This noisy, violent imagery cannot fail to conjure the sense of a battlefield in full flow.

Space is a salvo

If we are to accept the interpretation of the poem as a representation of the aggressive treatment of the Irish at the hands of invaders, it is interesting to consider the attitude the poetic voice adopts towards this invasion. Looking again at the opening line 'We are prepared', we gain a sense that this invasion is expected. Time and again the Irish have withstood the onslaught of attacks which have spanned the centuries. This idea is supported by the selection of adjective 'wizened' to describe the earth; whilst literally this is referring to the fact it is weather-beaten and therefore unable to produce crops, it could also almost personify the earth and refer to the accumulation of experience it has built up over time. The ongoing battles fought over this land cause it to know better than to produce fruit, as this would only be destroyed. This is a source of bitter comfort to the narrative voice; there are no 'stacks or stooks that can be lost', the sibilance here reinforcing the resentful tone, resigned to the idea that they cannot ever truly make this place a fruitful home. The crops could represent the cultural identity of the Irish, which is never allowed to truly flourish because time and again it is swept aside by invading forces.

Arguably personification of the trees continues this theme; Heaney dedicates seven of the poem's nineteen lines to the trees so they are clearly significant. Whilst crops can grow in a single season, trees take hundreds of years to take root and grow. The fact 'There are no trees' to 'provide company' or 'natural shelter' suggest a sense of exposure and isolation, a pervasive lack of protection. At the same time, their strength as a people has also prevented their enemy from taking root on their land also. Trees can 'raise a chorus in a gale' which can be seductive, and lead one to 'listen to that thing you fear' and 'forget' that 'it pummels your house too'. One interpretation of these lines is that when an enemy has occupied your land for a significant period, you can begin spend all your time lamenting its presence rather than doing something about it. Conversely, the threatening way in which listening here is linked with forgetting could reflect the idea that people can also be taken in by a quite different 'chorus', that of their occupying enemies. Significantly of course, 'there are no trees' on this island, a fact which is noted twice, both in line six and line twelve. The Irish, perhaps, are impervious to the seductive 'company' the 'chorus' of their enemy may attempt to provide, and offer no instrument upon which they can play their tune.

This notion is continued through several almost oxymoronic phrases throughout the remainder of the poem. The trees are compared to the sea which 'explode comfortably' against the cliffs. Once again, the reader is warned that they 'might think the sea is company'; the 'comfortable' nature of the explosions reflecting a sense that this is something they have become so accustomed to it has begun to feel a natural part of their everyday lives. There is something sinister in the juxtaposition of these terms - the idea that something as destructive as an explosion could begin to feel comforting is terrifying, as it is ultimately eroding their 'cliffs', the very edges of their homeland. The subsequent image is of the storm hitting their 'very windows', demonstrating how close the enemy has come to their homes 'like a tame cat turned savage'. Once again, a juxtapositioning of opposing ideas; a further warning that an enemy can appear 'tame', but will quickly turn 'savage' once it is allowed to reach your doorstep.

The final lines continue to present the destructive power of the enemy. But this time the violence is juxtaposed with a sense of emptiness: it 'strafes invisibly', 'space is a salvo' and we are 'bombarded by the empty air'. The 'huge nothing that we fear' reflects the sense that the enemy does not have to take a physical presence to wield destructive power. Continuing the idea described above relating to the seductive 'chorus' of the trees, perhaps

Heaney is exploring the constant attempts by the British, for surely it is the British who are the enemy here, to erode the cultural identity of the Irish, not simply through physical violence, but through the gradual erosion of their human rights and liberties, and the removal of power from Stormont to Westminster. Although Westminster did not fully remove all powers of the devolved Northern Irish government until 1972, Heaney lived through a time when there were extensive inequalities within the system and, as explained in the introduction, certainly felt that he was a victim of persecution as a Catholic growing up and living in Northern Ireland.

Subversive structures and structural subversions

Heaney chooses to adopt blank verse throughout the poem, which could be considered at odds with this interpretation. The use of five feet per line, with the rhythmic unstressed, stressed syllables has been adopted time and again by traditional English poets throughout history, from Shakespeare to Shelley, so it seems contrary for Heaney to adopt it here if it is to be considered to give voice to Irish sensibility oppressed by the British. However, there are many ways in which Heaney subverts this traditional English structure.

To begin with, if we look at the first foot 'We are' - is the stress really on the second syllable 'are', or does it fall more naturally on the first syllable 'We', creating a trochee rather than an iamb right from the start? This jar to the rhythm is repeated in the final line, which begins 'Strange, it' and the emphasis falls more naturally on the first word than the second. The irregular number of 19 lines is also at odds with more traditional poetic structures, such as the Shakespearean sonnet which has 14 lines. The odd number resists the neatness and regularity of traditional poetic forms, as does the use of half-rhymes at the beginning and the end. 'Squat' and 'slate' share consonant but not vowel sounds in lines one and two, mirroring the 'air' and 'fear' of the final two lines. It is almost as if Heaney is playing around with these traditional structures and bending them to suit his own purpose. This idea is reinforced by his use of informal 'as you can see' and 'you know what I mean', injecting a casual conversational tone into the formal structure.

Noticeably there's a lot of caesuras and enjambments in this solid, single block of a poem. Many sentences finish in the middle of lines (check where the full stops fall) and many others run over line endings and into the following line or lines. And it's not just the sentences that look like they've been knocked somewhat askew. Many of the fuller rhymes crop up in unusual places, not just at the ends of lines. Take the first rhyme word, 'squat', echoed in 'rock' and later more weakly in 'lost'. Or towards the end of the poem, the end rhyme 'hits' is picked up in the middle of the next line, in 'spits' and echoes again in 'sit'. Though the interior of the poem may be knocked about and out of shape, the overall form of the poem, its island of words, endures and retains its structural integrity.

Storm on an Island crunched:

We - good - wizened - hay - lost - company - blast - chorus - listen - forgetting - trees - company - comfortably - hits - windows - savage - invisibly - bombarded - nothing.

Carol Ann Duffy, *War Photographer*

In a famously distressing photograph from the Vietnam War a group of children are pictured running towards the camera and away from a napalm attack that has left the background of the photo a blaze of fire and smoke. [Napalm was an anti-personal weapon, a flammable liquid that stuck to the skin when it ignited.] To the left in the foreground a young boy's distraught expression conveys the horror and trauma of the attack. In the middle, a young, naked girl runs towards us, crying. She is clearly terrified and in agony, with napalm burns all over her body. Her burns were so bad doctors did not think she could possibly survive. Thankfully she did.

Imagine you are the photographer who took this picture. Whilst it might be a natural human instinct to immediately run to the aid of this young girl, it is your job to document these events as they unfold and report them as a neutral observer. Could you do a job like this, which requires you to suppress your empathy for the suffering of others? The image had far reaching consequences; the Western world were brought face-to-face with the devastating effect of Napalm on innocent civilians, and it helped fuel public opinion against the Vietnam war. The use of such a weapon is now against international law.

Carol Ann Duffy was inspired to write *War Photographer* due to her friendship with two well respected war photographers, Don McCullin and Philip Jones Griffiths. She was interested in the difficulties these men faced when they witnessed such horrific moments in human history and were forced to attempt to capture them for the 'consumption' of the media in the Western world. Whilst the Vietnam image may have inspired a public outcry in 1972, Duffy explores the notion that our sympathy for those depicted is fleeting, and the proliferation of images of war-torn nations has ultimately desensitised all or us to the extent that we simply 'do not care'.

The observer & the observed

Duffy has chosen to use a third person narrative perspective throughout, creating the impression that 'The War Photographer' of the title is the subject under scrutiny. There is a clear irony here, as the observer becomes the observed; the poetic voice scrutinises the intimate moments of the photographer in his dark room, revealing his inner turmoil as he 'is finally alone'.

The intimate knowledge the narrator has of the photographer's thoughts gives the reader the impression that the photographer's mind is turning inwards; he appears to be scrutinising his role in creating these 'spools of suffering' - the sibilance here perhaps reinforcing his sense of disgust. The fragmented sentence structures are like a stream of consciousness: 'Belfast. Beirut. Phnom Penh', as if his mind is flashing back to the war-torn locations almost involuntarily.

Ordinary pain

The sequence of flashbacks is brought to life with the final sentence of the first stanza 'all flesh is grass'. This is a much-quoted biblical phrase used to refer to the transitory nature of life: ultimately when we die our flesh is returned to the earth and feeds in to the cycle of life. Used in this context the image could reflect the way the photographer is attempting to comfort himself and rationalise the immense quantity of death he is witnessing. The reference to 'flesh' could refer to the nakedness of the victims (linking to the picture of the Vietnam girl); their indignity overwhelms him and covers the images quite literally like a landscape of grass. Reminding himself of this saying is an example of the way he attempts to separate his own emotional responses from what he is witnessing, but this becomes increasingly difficult as the poem progresses.

There is a juxtapositioning throughout the poem of the suffering experienced by the people in the war-torn communities and the mundane lives of those in 'Rural England'. Statements such as 'simple weather can dispel' our 'ordinary pain' and that the 'fields' of England don't 'explode beneath the feet of running children' emphasise the gulf between experiences. We take the peace and security of our land for granted, and the image of running children is particularly powerful in evoking a sense of the vulnerability and innocence of many of those caught up in these war zones. Once again, the Vietnam image of the running girl is evoked, particularly within the last phrase of the stanza: 'nightmare heat' with its suggestions of napalm. Coupled with the reference to flesh in the last phrase of the opening stanza, we cannot fail to make the connection with the burning skin of children. Duffy's use of imagery combined with careful structuring is hugely powerful and evocative, bringing home to the reader both what the civilians in battlegrounds experience, and how the war photographer struggles to cope with bearing witness to it.

Trembling & control

Duffy adopts the traditional iambic pentameter throughout most the poem, a metre often reserved for weighty and serious topics. However, there are key moments where she deviates from the pattern. Line two of stanza one, for example, contains an additional iamb, reflecting how the 'spools of suffering' are too great to be contained within the line. The line therefore becomes iambic hexameter, also known as an alexandrine. In line four of stanza one the opposite happens; only four iambs are used. In contrast to the over-spilling of suffering in line two, Duffy here could be highlighting the inadequacy the photographer feels his dark room offers as a place of sanctity to develop these images of the end of human life.

The four regular stanzas each consisting of exactly six lines reflect the photographer's desire to maintain order and control over his emotions. This idea is further evident in the 'ordered rows' he uses to lay out his images. The rhyme scheme is also regular, with a rhyming couplet in lines two and three and five and six of each stanza. However, the fact that lines one and four do not tie in with this neat, ordered pattern reflects that despite his best efforts, the photographer is not able to fully maintain regimented control, over suffering, over his emotions and over the effect of his photos. This ties in with the 'tremble' that creeps into his hands, as he attempts to remind himself that 'he has a job to do.'

The second stanza starts abruptly. A matter of fact tone is swiftly established, as the photographer attempts to jolt his mind back to the more mundane tasks of the present, where 'solutions slop in trays'. Again, however, the sibilance which creeps into this phrase highlights his disgust, and reveals the trembling of his hands. This time as he thinks of the present, the sentence fragment 'Rural England' also carries a sense of distaste, perhaps even bitterness. 'Home again' follows. Any comfort is, however very short-lived. Just a couple of metrical beats later and his mind turns to the contrast between the 'ordinary pain' felt here with the suffering felt by the 'running children' who are the subjects of his photographs.

The start of the third stanza contrasts with the start of the second. Whereas at that point he had been attempting to force himself to focus on the task at hand, this time the statement 'Something is happening' demonstrates that he has now been irrevocably drawn into the world of his photographs. The development of the photographs is of course what the photographer is aiming to do, but the process of the development of one picture in particular absorbs him completely; whilst the subject of the picture is a 'stranger' to him (the phrase perhaps highlighting the attitude he typically takes towards his subjects), the way in which he becomes a 'half-formed ghost' reflects the ghostly nature of the image, and hints towards the fact that he is no longer alive. This is confirmed as his mind turns to 'the cries of this man's wife' and how the 'blood stained into the foreign dust'.

They do not care

The final stanza acts as a moment of realisation for the war photographer; the pain of a single man in the previous stanza merge into 'a hundred agonies', emphasising that the shot he captured is a drop in the ocean of suffering he witnesses. Emotive language is juxtaposed with the more factual 'in black and white', bringing us to the perspective of his editor who merely sees the images as a product he is packaging for consumption within 'Sunday's supplement' of his paper. There is a bitterness in the subsequent reference to the reader's response, as although their 'eyeballs prick with tears', this is a fleeting moment quickly forgotten as they move on to their comfortable lives and their 'pre-lunch beers'. The trite internal rhyme reinforces the sense of the photographer's disdain. The narrative perspective finally brings us back to the point of view of the photographer who gazes 'impassively', emotionally disconnected, out of the aeroplane window at his own country where 'they do not care' about his work nor the suffering he is paid to witness for us.

War Photographer crunched:

Finally – suffering – red – church – priest – flesh – job –
tremble – home – dispel – explode – nightmare – happening –
twist – ghost – approval – must – blood – agonies – editor –
supplement – beers – impassively – care.

Carol Rumens, *The Émigree*

Whilst most the poems within this anthology could be considered reflective of each poet's personal experience, *The Émigrée* serves an important reminder that the poetic voice or speaker is not necessarily the poet's own voice. Often poets create characters which offer a different perspective, to allow them to explore and empathise with different experiences. Born in London, a city which Rumens describes as 'the city of her heart', the poet did not emigrate there, so this poem is not strictly speaking autobiographical in the way Agard's *Checking Out Me History* might be. Though it is possible to read the poem metaphorically and consider the country referred to as a person, or a time that has been lost, for the purposes of this analysis we will focus on the city as a physical place.

Rumens describes writing as 'a conversation - with my parents, with myself, with the living, with the dead, with friends, with strangers, and perhaps with words themselves.' Given that she lived for many years in London, a city with a diverse and multicultural population, she is likely to have had many 'conversations' with people who have emigrated to the UK, particularly those from war-torn countries. This poem offers an homage to people displaced from their homelands, sympathising with their pain and the conflict exile creates within them. 'Émigrée' is the feminine form of the French term for a woman who has emigrated, and the term has connotations of political or social exile, meaning that the person has left their homeland to escape persecution.

An impression of sunlight

A strong juxtaposition of lexis runs throughout the poem; on the one hand, there is a range of positive and beautiful images of light, used about the city: 'sunlight-clear', 'white streets', 'graceful slopes glow', 'shining eyes'. These images create the impression the place occupies a privileged place in the narrator's memory; it has been romanticised as somewhere with almost religious significance, its heavenly qualities suggested by the repeated references to light. On the other hand, the narrator explains that she has been 'branded' by the 'impression of sunlight', creating a sense of violence and force; her childhood experiences will remain with her forever. Branding takes place to symbolise ownership, sickeningly used within the  slave trade and on animals, burning away the skin to make a permanent mark. The narrator feels that the sunlight of her homeland has created a burning and permanent mark on her psyche, one that can be painful to remember and can never be erased.

References to violence are repeated throughout the poem, building up the heart-breaking story of the narrator's home country that she has been forced to leave behind physically, but cannot leave behind psychologically. The  opening stanza states that the city 'may be at war, it may be sick with tyrants', but 'the worst news I receive of it cannot break my original view' which is 'the bright, filled paperweight'. The personification of the city as suffering from an illness demonstrates the perversion the 'tyrants' have created within her homeland. If we consider the early 90s, when Rumens published the poem in her anthology *Thinking of Skins,* there are many countries this story could apply to: Sierra Leone, Liberia, El Salvador, Guatemala, Nicaragua, to name a few. Each of these places suffered civil wars in which, it could be argued tyrannical leaders oppressed their people. Revolutionary uprisings followed and the massacre of thousands, often innocent civilians. Unfortunately, Rumens' poem is just as relevant today, in Syria, Afghanistan, Yemen and many other places. Perhaps it is because of the devastating range of conflicts which stretch throughout history and will stretch into the future that Rumens chose to make the country within the poem both anonymous and timeless. Any émigrée could take her poem's words for their own, as it speaks both to them and for them, so that others may gain some insight into the devastating impact of such an experience.

Despite the illness the country is suffering, the narrator still views it in the way she did as a child, and the image of the 'bright, filled paperweight' evokes the sense of childhood fascination with a magical object emitting beauty and light. The image of the city contained within the paperweight could represent the way it has become contained within her mind, a magical and enduring presence. Once again, however, the description is a double-edged sword: it may be radiant, perhaps heavenly, but it is a weight, and one she must bear forever. It's memory weighs on her heart as 'time rolls its tanks', a destructive metaphor delivered with harsh alliterative 't's, highlighting her bitterness as time moves on and conflict marches onwards with it. Towards the end of the poem she states that the city walls 'mutter death', echoing the lives that have been lost through this state of never-ending conflict.

The form and structure of the poem could also be said to represent the internal discord of emotions the émigrée feels about her city. Rumens has chosen to use italics throughout, which gives the impression of internal thought, a stream of consciousness, almost like a dream, reflecting the sense that the poem is a childhood memory. This effect is reinforced by repeated use of enjambment, and the lack of any regular rhyme scheme. The rhythm also does not fully establish itself; there tends to be five stresses to each line, but this is not strictly adhered to, particularly as the poem progresses. While the stanzas may appear regular on the surface, on closer inspection the third has an extra line. This reflects the overall lack of control and regularity throughout the poem; in a similar way to *Exposure*, arguably it reflects how the émigrée attempts to give an impression of control, but beneath this surface lies a sense of unease and discord.

I can't get it off my tongue

Despite the impression, we gain of the émigrée leaving her homeland in early childhood, and therefore learning another language from a young age, her mother tongue appears to influence her mastery of the new vernacular, causing her to 'spill' a 'grammar'. This childish phrase reinforces the idea that she is not completely at home in this new land, but her 'child's vocabulary' is 'like a hollow doll', so her original language is not truly her own anymore either. The simile has an ominous feel, as though the words she used in

her childhood are now empty; she is left carrying around a shell which only has echoes of meaning which haunt her ability to communicate.

At this point the sense that she is a political exile from her homeland, and that her people face persecution is emphasised; her mother tongue is described now as 'a lie, banned by the state', suggesting that the language of her people has been outlawed, a practice employed often by those wishing to oppress those viewed as enemies. Eradicating a language takes a systematic dismantling of education and administration systems, further demonstrating that the conflict the émigrée has escaped from spans significant periods of time, and that its consequences are far reaching. Despite this, she still 'can't get it off [her] tongue', it 'tastes of sunlight'; once again the juxtaposition of the positive and the negative reinforce the sense that her feelings are deeply, intimately conflicted. The heavenly qualities of the place implied by 'sunlight' are ones that she attempts to cast aside, but the tactile imagery of taste suggests that all her senses are permanently influenced by her experience; it affects her entire being, her homeland is an integral part of her sense of self.

The final stanza of the poem further explores the conflicted relationship she has with her homeland. While she says 'I comb its hair and love its shining eyes', an image suggesting maternal love and care she feels towards its memory, the memory soon turns as the city becomes one of 'walls' which 'accuse me of absence' and threateningly 'circle me'. Once again positive memories entrap her; in this case, she is encircled by them and trapped within them, a metaphor which encapsulates all her previous feelings. She is held captive within a prison of her memories, memories which begin optimistically but soon turn 'dark'. Ultimately her 'shadow' 'falls as evidence of sunlight', and whilst Rumens' decision to end the poem with this positive word could suggest hope, a shadow is a part of yourself that will always follow you and can never be cast aside.

They accuse me

The final stanza of the poem also provides an insight into the émigrée's feelings about her new home, feelings which are very relevant to migrants to this country today. The Syrian crisis has led to more and more refugees attempting to make Britain their home, but the reception they have received from many has been shamefully hostile. The narrator seems to conflate the images of her original city and the city of her new country; suddenly, the 'walls' which 'accuse' her of absence take on the pronoun 'they', which is repeated in the final line where 'they' accuse her of 'being dark in their free city'. The accusations echo the sentiments of elements of the British press, which adopt an accusing tone when referring to the increasing number of refugees seeking asylum in Britain.

The émigrée feels she is shamed for not being in her home city, not only by her city itself, but also by the walls of her new city, which could also feel like a prison. The almost childish phrase 'they circle me' evokes bullying. 'They mutter death' becomes ever-more threatening: not only do the walls speak the deaths of her people, but the harsh sounding verb 'mutter' suggests whispered threats from hostile people who surround her in 'their free city'. This place belongs to them, the freedom in this country belongs to them; they are not prepared to share it with her and so she must go on living in her prison. At this point, the final image of her shadow could perhaps offer her some comfort: it is evidence she exists as a person within her own right, it is evidence that, despite these dark times, she still has at her core the wisdom that her homeland is part of her, and, despite the pain and anguish it causes, no one will ever take this away.

The Émigrée crunched:

Country - sunlight-clear - seems - city - break - paperweight - tyrants - branded - sunlight - graceful - tanks - frontiers - vocabulary - hollow - coloured - banned - sunlight - passport - white - docile -shining - walls - circle - accuse - mutter - shadow.

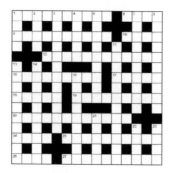

Imtiaz Dharker, *Tissue*

Not a crossword puzzle

It's a curious poem this one by Dharker, a poem that doesn't give too much away and makes the reader work quite hard. And even when we do work hard to decode the meanings we may still be left with a sense of mystery. Surely, of course, this is deliberate. A poem is more than a series of messages dressed up on obscure language to be cracked like a crossword puzzle. Dharker makes sure we do not have quite enough information to dispel the mystery. Take the first stanza, for instance. The poet proposes that thin 'paper that lets light through' is what 'could alter things'. The phrasing deliberately frustrates interpretation: The verb 'could' is not definite, but conditional; 'alter' begs the question in what ways, and, in particular, the noun 'things' is intentionally non-specific. What 'things' we might reasonable enquire of the poet 'could be' 'altered' by this paper?

Indeed, readers might reasonably expect the following stanzas to shed light on this puzzling opening proposition. But instead we are given multiple examples of the type of paper the poet has in mind, old paper, map paper, shop paper. The key quality of each of these papers appears to be that they let light through in one way or another, but the poet does not illuminate us with what this action could alter or how it could do so. The introduction of a new character, 'the architect' into a poem about paper promises some delayed explanation. But, once again, our decoding instincts are thrown off the scent by a comparison of building with bricks and with paper. The poem concludes with a second shift - the sudden introduction of a previously hidden you and a development of the tissue paper – skin metaphor.

In short, we never get a clear resolution to the opening proposition. Either we can stamp our feet in frustration and throw the poem into the recycling bin in disgust, or we can puzzle away at it a bit more and see where that gets us. As we are English students let us try the latter.

A structure never meant to last

The fragility of life and everything within it is a point of fascination for Dharker, explored here and famously in her poem *The Temporary Face* in which the narrative voice explains 'I learn to love/ the thing that has to be erased/ the thing I may not be allowed to keep/ sand that runs away beneath my running feet'. Whilst these lines offer what may have been a child's perspective on the fleeting nature of those things she may not be 'allowed' to keep forever, *Tissue* has the authoritative tone of a narrator who has experienced much of life and can reflect on the vast range of human experience. Dharker's use of unrhymed quatrains without a regular metre helps to create the impression of free thought or musings upon life, a stream of consciousness which is also created by the repeated enjambment.

The opening reference to 'paper that lets the light shine through' creates an image of wisdom, with light potentially referring to understanding and knowledge, or even having religious significance with the light referring to God. It is interesting that the light does not come from the paper itself; instead the paper acts as a mechanism through which light can shine. It is 'paper thinned by age or touching' which could 'alter things'. So once the paper has lived through a significant period and experience it can 'shed light' and offer wisdom to those who choose to read it. This image appears to offer potential, and the sense that whatever it could 'alter' will bring about positive change. Perhaps if people choose to listen to the wisdom of those things that have the benefit of age an experience then their lives will be changed for the better. The final line of the poem 'turned into your skin' completes the extended metaphor, making a clear link between the paper in the opening stanza that could offer a means to access wisdom, and the human skin which also thins with age and experience. There is a sense of finality about this concluding line: once your skin turns to this thin 'transparent' tissue, you are able to offer wisdom and light, but you are near the end of life. Transparency could link to the idea that you are almost invisible, soon to disappear into the 'light' forever, with the light once again evoking religious imagery, perhaps suggestive of the afterlife.

Well-used books...maps too

The wide variety of uses for paper are listed throughout the poem through a series of images, each linking back to the idea that the paper is 'thinned by age or touching', 'transparent with attention', 'smoothed and stroked / and thinned to be transparent'. The documents include those which apparently hold great power, such as the Koran which contains the 'names and histories' of 'who was born to whom / the height and weight, who / died where and how, on which sepia date'. It is clear that we, as humans, place much emphasis on this record keeping, but the asyndetic listing here creates the endless sense that perhaps we record too much, and not those things that are important. The way in which this list not only adopts  enjambment from line to line but from one stanza to another between 'whom' and 'the height' adds the impression that this is a lengthy process, the pace is slowed, forcing the reader to take pause over the list. The trite internal rhyme between 'weight' and 'date' also generates the sense that Dharker is mocking this record keeping and trivialising the endless hours spent over it. The present participle verbs 'smoothing' and 'stroking' add to the sense that the poet is mocking our obsession with paper and the almost unhealthy attraction we have to it.

'Maps too.' are added later, almost as an afterthought, but in this stanza the light has even more prominence as 'The sun shines through / their borderlines, the marks / that rivers make, roads, / railtracks, mountainfolds'. The visual imagery here highlights that as humans, we can document the natural world around us, perhaps in an attempt to gain power over it, but our attempts are futile as ultimately the paper will fade and the sun will have dominance over every element of our diligent records. The subsequent stanza abruptly adds 'Fine slips from grocery shops' to continue the list of

marks made on the map, which almost trivialises this document and places it on an equal footing with the paper used every day for receipts. The mocking tone of the list in this stanza mirrors the list of facts recorded in the Koran, with the reference to 'what was paid by credit card' injecting a jarring image of modernity into the sense of timelessness that had been evoked. The fact they 'might fly our lives like paper kites' creates the ominous impression that we have allowed paper to control us, and it is important to read this image carefully. On first reading it may seem that the receipts are flying through the air, but it is actually the 'fine slips' which are the ones with the agency: it is they who have hold of the kites, and it is our lives that are controlled by them. This is a disturbing picture of modern life, with humans fluttering in the wind without any direction, anchored down by their debts and the paper records of them.

Let the daylight break...

The transient nature of man-made objects is repeated in Dharker's reference to buildings. Whilst it is more difficult to determine their fragility, if they were made of paper it would be easier to 'see how easily / they fall away on a sigh, a shift / in the direction of the wind'. The poet appears to be exploring a similar idea to Shelley in *Ozymandias*, in that great structures can be worn away by time and the force of nature. This comparison extends to the reference to the 'shapes that pride can make'; clearly the king in *Ozymandias* felt pride in his constructions which did not stand the test of time, but Dharker seems to be

taking this a step further, referring to all the material creations of man as less important than what we should be aiming for: 'a way to trace a grand design / with living tissue'.

The ironic reference to a 'grand design' at first appears to link to semantic field of architecture and construction used up until that point 'build again', 'brick or block', 'capitals and monoliths', but the break between the stanzas builds suspense before the true meaning is revealed, that we should be building with 'living tissue'. We should realise that our lives our 'never meant to last', perhaps referring to man's obsession with gaining a place in history, demonstrated through endless recording of dates, and maps, and constructing 'monoliths' which will outlive them. The irony is that even these records and buildings will eventually give way to the test of time, so these efforts are futile. Dharker appears to be pleading with the reader to 'let the daylight break through': allow the wisdom and understanding into your lives so that you do not waste any more time over these futile endeavours. Instead, concentrate on building a 'grand design with living tissue', focus on the living and actually living, as you were 'never meant to last'.

Cracking the puzzle?

So, did we manage it? Though the poem never makes crystal clear exactly what the 'thing' was that 'could' be 'altered' by paper it does allow us to reach a tentative reading. The 'thing' is ourselves or our lives and it/ we can be transformed by understanding our impermanence and fragility, by not trying to build our lives with bricks and blocks and most of all, by allowing light to shine through us.

Tissue crunch:

Paper – shine – alter – age – well-used – Koran – histories – born who – date – smoothed – transparent – paper – drift – fall – wind shines – marks – make – mountainfolds – slips – sold – credit –card – kites – architect – layer – script – build – daylight – monolith – pride – design – tissue – last – smoothed – transparent – skin.

Simon Armitage, *Remains*

According to Judith Lewis Herman, 'the conflict between the will to deny horrible events and the will to proclaim them aloud is the central dialectic of psychological trauma'. It is this trauma that is undeniably at the heart of Armitage's poem; originally published in the 2008 collection *The Not Dead*, *Remains* is one of a series of poems that seek to understand and convey the mentality of British soldiers after returning from wars overseas. Based on actual interviews with three returned soldiers, Armitage observed that 'most of the poems I wrote revolved around a key 'flashback' scene, requiring each soldier to revisit the very incident he was desperately hoping to forget' and it is easy to see the marks of Post-Traumatic Stress Disorder within *Remains* as the soldier struggles to come to terms with the fallout of taking a life.

We get sent out

We join our speaker mid-conversation, in what first appears to be another casual tale in a series of stories. We have no idea what's come before – we are thrown into the story *in media res* – which is important both because it reflects the significance of this particular moment to the soldier, and also because it denies the reader an opportunity to understand the context of the situation. We, like the soldier later reveals himself to be, are trapped in this moment, and can only draw out meaning from the images we are presented with.

At first glance, it is easy to dismiss the soldier's easy anecdotal opening and conversational tone as evidence that conflict and violence have become normal, everyday things to the speaker – after all, this is simply 'another occasion'. The soldier's speech is composed of casual, off-hand and colloquial language; hence it appears that this is just another story to tell down the pub. He talks of how they 'get sent out', of 'one of his mates', of shooting as 'letting fly', of a body being 'carted off'. Although we know that the speaker is really there to handle a potentially violent robbery, the use of the verb 'tackle' also lulls us into a false sense of familiarity. The use of a word so heavily associated with sports such as football and rugby – with *games* – serves as a euphemism that distances us from the brutal reality of the situation. The continued use of colloquial expressions such as 'legs it' and phrases that mimic the rhythm of conversation ('well myself and somebody else and somebody else') further obscures the harshness of what is really happening, to the point that it is genuinely shocking when the three soldiers 'open fire'. And the transition from ordinary to horrific happens so fast, in just a few lines into the poem, mimicking the way the situation escalated suddenly. There is a sharp contrast between the ordinary, conversational tone and the extreme violence of the situation, a sense that this is just another day at the office and the soldier is completely divorced from, perhaps numbed by, the reality of his actions.

This impression is reinforced by the callous way in which the soldier describes the treatment of the body afterwards. The looter is treated with a shocking lack of respect that likens him to rubbish; there is no moment of consideration for the fact that the soldiers have just taken a human life. Instead, one of the soldiers simply 'tosses his guts back into his body' and the looter is then 'carted off in the back of a lorry'. The looter is seemingly easily disposable, the speaker's use of colloquial verbs such as 'tossed' and 'carted off' imply this is an everyday occurrence. Violence has become normalised and human life has become devalued – the soldier simply no longer cares. Notice too how that telling phrase about whether the looter was 'probably armed, possibly not' is repeated in the poem. It's a crucial detail; did the soldiers mow down an unarmed man or not? But the verse passes swiftly over it as if this crucial legal and moral question is almost an irrelevance.

Near the knuckle

Whilst the first half of the poem makes it easy to dismiss the speaker as an unfeeling cog in the war machine, and to chalk the poem up to yet another commentary on the harsh reality of conflict, the final four stanzas clearly show the long-lasting effects this event has on the soldier's psyche. Haunted by the looter's death, the soldier's own life seems to come to a standstill, forever locked in a nightmare moment he cannot escape. The true tragedy here is not that the soldier does not feel guilt, but that he is unable to articulate these feelings.

Trauma is paradoxical in nature – there is a tension between the constant return to the repressed (or unwanted) memory and the inability to fully express it in a way that renders it whole. In *Remains*, the soldier is trapped in

the horror of the moment, but never able to truly articulate his feelings. He lacks the vocabulary that would allow him to express himself, instead falling back on more familiar colloquial phrases from everyday life. The references to sport ('tackle') and poker ('three of a kind') are not meant to suggest that the speaker sees war as a game. Instead they show his inability to fully comprehend and process what has happened – he must relate the terrible events of that day to safer, more recognisable experiences.

Armitage's poem is a dramatic monologue and there are, notably, almost two voices within the poem. The calm, conversational, surface voice speaks with mostly informal phrases; underneath it, between the lines is a starker, more emotional voice that expresses the soldier's true revulsion. This is most clearly seen in the second and third stanzas, where the recollection of the actual shooting seems to throw the speaker into a horrifying flashback. Whilst casually introduced with the colloquial phrasing of 'three of a kind all letting fly', the fallout of the soldier's actions is initially expressed through a violent metaphor that shockingly contrasts with the tone of the first two stanzas. Suddenly, the violence becomes all too real: 'I see every round as it rips through his life'. The language here is brutally clear; a string of monosyllabic words full of sharp consonants, the alliterative 'r's' echoing the ripping apart of both the looter's and the soldier's lives, the single plosive 'p' imitating the sound of a single gunshot. The horror of the memory is overwhelming; almost immediately, the soldier retreats into the familiarity of his casual phrasing: 'so we've hit this looter a dozen times'. His description of the man's body being 'sort of inside out' is almost childish, the addition of 'sort of' clearly reflecting his inability to express himself, yet this makes it even more horrific.

End of

The opening line of the fifth stanza is also brutal, but this time in its bitter irony. One of the few sentences that remains contained within a single line, with a full stop at the end, its real purpose is to show us that, despite his determination to put the incident squarely behind him, this story can never truly end for the soldier. The looter's life is over. The soldier's mission is over. But the soldier will never be able to fully escape the memories of what he has done. This is the volta, the turning point of the poem. Here we begin to fully realise the long-lasting, traumatic impact these events have had upon the soldier.

The 'blood-shadow' of the looter 'stays on the street', something that the soldier must 'walk right over [...] week after week'. Whilst this image serves as a neat visual reminder of the man's death, it also mirrors how the soldier will be haunted by his memories. The repetition of 'week after week' creates the illusion of an endless amount of time, foreshadowing the years that the soldier will suffer, whilst the compression of the two nouns clearly and concisely demonstrates the effect the looter's death will have upon the soldier. Just as a shadow constantly follows us wherever we go, so too will the soldier be haunted by the guilt he feels and the metaphorical blood on his hands.

Armitage further emphasises this lingering trauma by immediately following the image of the 'blood-shadow' with the soldier's return 'home on leave'. Whilst the short, simple sentence, ending mid-line, suggests that the soldier optimistically thinks that the 'story' will end with his return home and he'll be able to forget about it, the reality is near instantly revealed. To the soldier's horror, he only has to 'blink /and he bursts again through the doors of the bank'. The flashback is harsh and sudden; the plosive alliteration in 'But I blink', 'bursts' and 'bank' highlights how the explosive force of the memory. The effect is enhanced by the preceding caesura, which emphasises the suddenness of its onset. From one 'blink' to the next, the soldier is helplessly caught in his own memory, the enjambment reflecting the horror he cannot escape; just as the line continues across the two stanzas, the memory of the looter's death has followed the soldier home.

Armitage's soldier clearly cannot cope with the memory of his actions, torn apart by his inner turmoil in much the same way as the looter was 'torn apart by a dozen rounds'. Trapped in his own memories, he is doomed to endlessly repeat the events of that day as is shown through the poem's almost cyclical nature. The image of the bank, the ripped apart body and the 'dozen' shots from the first half of the poem are repeated, as is the line 'probably armed, possibly not'. The soldier is haunted by possibilities, constantly trying to justify his actions. Even the penultimate line, 'but near to the knuckle, here and now' maintains the same rhythm as 'probably armed, possibly not', suggesting that there is no escape from these distressing memories for the soldier even by the end of the poem.

Whilst the desperate admittance that the 'drinks and the drugs won't flush him out' is by itself a tragic confession of the soldier's state of mind, the use of the word 'flush' – a word often associated with hunting, and the flushing out of prey – suggests that the soldier has become truly vulnerable and is unable to process and control his violent memories. The looter is 'dug in behind enemy lines', a metaphor for how the memory of his death refuses to be brushed away. Once again, the soldier can only articulate his emotions in familiar phrases; however, here he must fall back on the language of soldiery rather than colloquial sayings, perhaps hinting that the soldier's traumatic flashbacks are increasingly distancing him from the normal and everyday.

Superficially the poem looks orderly, regular and composed. Seven fairly even quatrains finish with a final neat couplet. Examine it more closely, however and this appearance of control is revealed to be misleading. Take the rhyming, for instance: Though rhymes do crop up in the poem from time to time, often in pairs ['round'/'ground'; 'myself'/'somebody else'; 'mind'/'times'] and sometimes in triplets ['street'/'weeks'/'sleep'] they appear in odd, unexpected places, as if the rhyme pattern has been knocked askew. This impression is enhanced by the frequent use of pararhymes, such as 'lorry'/'story' and 'blink'/'bank'. Add to this the lack of a regular governing metre and it becomes clear that the impression of control and compose is superficial and hides internal disarray. Clearly too this pattern embodies the impression the soldier gives of himself. Outwardly he might appear to be fine, but internally things are very different indeed.

Gradually, as we progress through the poem, we see, in fact, how the soldier loses more and more control – slowly, at first, but then with ever increasing rapidity. With particularly traumatic moments highlighted through plosives and dashes right from the start, moments of terror breaking through the faux-casual control of the soldier's words, the pacing of the poem picks up after the soldier returns home on leave. The poem ends with one single continuous sentence that runs for seven lines, across three stanzas, a constant stream of enjambment that mirrors the soldier's ongoing pain and the endless repetition of his flashbacks. The list of sibilant adjectives describing the 'distant, sun-stunned, sand-smothered land' is nearly explosive. Violent compound adjectives express the soldier's state of mind and how he himself feels suffocated by his memories. Like the unusually long line, the speaker's own mind is unravelling and losing control; by the end of the poem, the standard four-line stanza format has been shattered and the poem ends in a simple non-rhymed couplet, representing the fracturing of the soldier's own sense of self.

And somebody else and somebody else

Armitage set out to explore the effect of war on soldiers and *Remains* clearly succeeds in showing the destruction war wreaks upon those who participate in it. Even the title is as divided. Clearly it refers to the human remains of the looter, but also too to how this memory remains in the psyche of the soldier. Moreover, the title suggests that the soldier is himself also now missing some part of himself; he is also the remains of this brutal experience. And this unnamed soldier is an everyman figure. Armitage could have added specific details to tie this story to a specific war, such as the war in Iraq. The fact that he doesn't do this signals the fact that he wanted to get at something universal about the experience of conflict. The anonymous narrator thus embodies the way in which abuse and trauma is passed on and carried over from one situation to another.

Whilst the cyclical nature of the poem embodies his inability to escape his memories, it is also notable that the entire poem is told in present tense. The soldier is trapped in one moment in time, unable to move on. Nowhere is this clearer than in the third stanza, where Armitage's use of anaphora highlights how the trauma is ongoing for the speaker. By repeating 'I see' at the beginning of the two lines, Armitage emphasises the pain and horror of the moment, showing that it is a vision that can never go away.

The poem takes on a confessional air. There is a distinct sense that the speaker sets out to comfort himself by sharing blame. The poem begins with the first-person plural 'we', suggesting a collective responsibility. It is not the soldier alone who decides to shoot: it is 'myself and somebody else and somebody else', who are explicitly described as being 'all of the same mind'. Repetitive listing implies a desperation to share the responsibility for his actions, further emphasised by the almost superfluous repetition of 'all' no less than three times in a single stanza. But as soon as the shots have been fired, the narrative switches to the first person singular 'I'. With the exception of a single 'we've', the rest of the poem focuses exclusively on the speaker and his own personal guilt, culminating as the soldier finds himself completely responsible for the man's death: 'his bloody life in my bloody hands'.

His bloody life in my bloody hands

There are echoes of Lady Macbeth here, haunted to madness by guilt and the metaphorical blood on her hands; a particularly striking image that ends the poem. Earlier still, we are reminded of Macbeth after the murder of Duncan with the emphasis placed on 'Sleep' and 'Dream' in the sixth stanza. Both words begin their respective lines, separated by caesurae, lending them focus. Just as Macbeth's violent actions 'doth murder sleep', so too do the soldier's. These emphasised words can even be linked to Hamlet's famous soliloquy as he muses over whether 'to sleep, perchance to dream'; here, the Danish prince's reflections over the afterlife and what awaits us there seem a remarkably apt concern for the soldier. With such a vivid sense of tragedy in *Remains*, it is easy to see the after-images of these characters within Armitage's traumatised soldier. If he can share nothing else with his victim, he shares the blood and in the poem's final couplet looter and soldier are fused inseparably together.

Although Armitage vividly depicts the brutal effects of conflict, this is not a poem dedicated to attacking the idea of war. Instead, it invites us to empathise with those who fight and to try to understand what they must live with. The soldier's colloquial phrasing, with his chatty tone and frequent use of contractions, draws us in and allows us to connect with his thought processes in a way that is perhaps impossible with the more rigidly controlled structures of other conflict poetry. Armitage's soldier develops an authentic voice that we can recognise. He is a real and, most importantly, human insight into the realities of war and its after-effects. As Armitage points out, 'for traumatized soldiers, the harrowing images and accompanying feelings persist, in some cases for a lifetime.' This poem does not judge the soldier's actions as right or wrong; what it does is allow us to gain that little bit of extra insight into this eternal issue.

Remains crunched:

Tackle – legs it – probably – possibly – all – I – rips – looter – dozen – agony – tosses – guts – carted off – story – blood-shadow – blink – bursts – sleep – flush – head – dug in – enemy – sun-stunned – sand-smothered – bloody.

John Agard, *Checking Out Me History*

Blind me to me own identity

Imagine growing up in a world where you are only ever taught the history of another nation; the historical figures were born more than seven thousand miles away and the events bear no real relevance to your own ancestry. You might feel pretty angry about this, correct? Well that's exactly how John Agard feels, and this anger emanates from the page in this poem. Agard often writes with a passionate, heart-felt tone, which is best conveyed when you listen to him performing his poetry aloud. His poetry offers a means through which he can express his hostility towards the treatment he and his ancestors have received because of the colonial rule of Britain within Guiana, and echoes the sentiments of many postcolonial writers whose identity has been threatened by the wilful ignorance of this cultural domination.

Repetition of the punchy phrase 'Dem tell me' initiates an angry tone from the outset; the repetition creates a sense of outrage and disbelief. The second line's emphasis on a *'dem'* and the *'me'*, questions the right of whoever 'dem' are to inform the poet of anything. The historical accuracy of what he is told is called into question when Agard says he is told what 'dem want' to tell him, as if his teachers invent whatever information suited their purposes at the time. The metaphorical reference to the way they 'bandage up' his eyes suggests he is deliberately prevented from seeing the truth, deliberately 'blind[ed]' to his 'own identity'.

Bitterness is echoed in the rhyme scheme. A sing-song chanting rhythm is generated, with the end of each line linking to the one before, building into a crescendo of anger. Events he is informed of by are trivialised by referring, offhandedly to the clichéd '1066 and all dat', rhyming tritely with 'Dick Whittington and he cat'. Linking a key historical moment in Western history (the Battle of Hastings) with a nursery rhyme about a cat reduces the significance of the historical events he was taught, because, of course, to him they had no relevance or significance, taking place in a land so far away. This pattern is repeated from line 11, where 'de man who discover de balloon' is rhymed with 'de cow who jump over de moon' and 'de dish ran away with de spoon'. There is a dark humour about these rhymes, as if the situation might be laughable if it weren't for the fact that the history excluded to make room for this nonsense is his own history.

dem never tell me bout dat

Agard sets apart his own history structurally within the poem by using italics, clearly demonstrating how special these words are, suggesting perhaps that these words should be spoken differently, or perhaps sung in a celebratory style. They are in stark contrast to the angry tone of the previous lines, with the harsh consonant sounds of 'dat' rhyming with 'cat' and 'dat' again. Toussaint L'Ouverture's name is introduced in between these harsh rhymes and is set apart from them; clearly Agard feels differently about this historical figure, the only former slave to successfully

110

lead a black rebellion, the Haitian Revolution. The description of Toussaint uses a lexical field of strength and power: he has 'vision', he 'lick back Napoleon battalion', 'thorn to de French', 'de beacon of de Haitian Revolution'. Rhyming here is much more powerful and rhythmic, like a battle chant rather than the trite, bitter tones of the rhymes surrounding it.

The structural use of italics is repeated as the poem progresses as Agard refers to more and more historical figures. Those he views as his own are almost exclusively given the celebratory italics; those he feels were irrelevant  to him are referred to in disparaging terms. Nanny of the Maroons, or 'Nanny de maroon', as Agard refers to her, is a Jamaican national hero, an 18th century leader who escaped slavery and led her people to a free and peaceful existence. Once again, a lexical field of strength and power is used in her description: she was a 'see-far woman' of a 'mountain dream', meaning she had a vision of a future which was very difficult to achieve, like a mountain, but she was a 'fire-woman' whose 'struggle' led her people up a 'hopeful stream' to 'freedom river'; an exceptional achievement in times of slavery, demonstrating how hard her people fought under her visionary leadership.

But, as a child, Agard never got to hear her story, or those of others relevant to him. He was told about 'Lord Nelson and Waterloo', when he needed to hear about 'Shaka de great Zulu', and from this point onwards in the poem a fast-paced tirade of historical references pours onto the page, the rhyming quatrains continuing to build the diatribe. 'Columbus and 1492' is juxtaposed with 'de Caribs and de Arawaks too'; 'Florence Nightingale and she lamp', 'how Robin Hood used to camp' and the 'merry ole soul' of 'ole King Cole' contrast with the untold story of 'Mary Seacole'. Once again, rhyming creates ridicule; it is like his history has been crushed under the weight of the sheer number of historical dates, facts, and mythical figures enshrined in nursery rhymes, and his own history has been buried underneath. The story of Mary Seacole, a black nurse in the Crimean War, however, comes bursting forth - he will not allow this story to be buried and silenced any longer. Again, lexis of power and strength is repeated through this refrain 'she volunteer to go...even when de British said no'. She was 'brave', a 'healing star' and a 'yellow sunrise / to the dying'. Clearly here is a woman whose story had more relevance to the poet than the white Florence Nightingale did, and certainly more relevance than the merry soul of old King Cole.

All three historical figures which appear in these italicised refrains have references to light within their descriptions: 'Touissant de beacon', Nanny the 'fire-woman' and Seacole the 'healing star'. Not only does this refer to their visionary ability to provide a guiding light to those around them when they were alive, but it demonstrates Agard's feeling that they have all shed light on his ancestry and therefore his own sense of identity, the light representing the wisdom and understanding he has gained from learning about their existence.

carving out me identity

This is a passionate, defiant poem. Agard's use of Caribbean dialect, phonetic spelling and disregard for 'correct' rules of English grammar express this defiance. Repeated use of 'dem' rather than them, 'me' rather than 'my', 'bout' rather than 'about', 'dat' instead of 'that' to name just a few examples, allows the reader to re-create the voice of Agard, as if he is reading it aloud to us. The language we use is part of who we are, part of our cultural identity. Agard uses his own dialect within his poetry to pay homage to his roots; it would be incongruous to his message to write in Standard English and remove all these nuances of speech which, in themselves, go towards creating his sense of self. Rejecting Standard English is the stylistic analogue of rejecting what we might call Standard History.

The final line of the poem states the final act of defiance, and the rhythm, rhyme and tone of all the lines up until this point have been building to this ultimate crescendo. Anger radiates from the violent image he creates of 'carving', but there's also a strong sense of purpose, and of himself as the master and creator of his own identity. Carving is an artistic endeavour, which can create something beautiful and permanent, if the right care and attention is paid to it. The lines leading up to this final point repeat the opening refrain 'dem tell me', but this time he has an answer for 'dem'. Now he is older he is 'checking out' his 'own history'; the sense of agency is placed with him - he has the power and control to decide what he studies and learns. This is a final act of defiance towards whoever 'dem' are - his teachers, the government who set the curriculum, the British colonial masters of old. More than this, however, it feels like an exciting invitation. The informal 'checking out' could be an invitation to others, particularly young people, to 'check out' their own histories, and to take control of 'carving out' *their* own identity, to empower and enlighten themselves, as the poet has done.

Checking Out Me History crunched:

Dem - dem - tell - bandage – identity - all dat - cat - toussaint - never - toussaint - slave - vision - lick - napoleon - battalion - first - republic - thorn - french - beacon - revolution - balloon - moon - spoon - maroon - nanny - see-far - dream - fire-woman - hopeful - freedom - waterloo - zulu - 1492 - de arawaks - nightingale - hood - cole - seacole - jamaica - travel - crimean - volunteer - british - brave - star - wounded - sunrise - dying - me - me - own – identity.

Jane Weir, *Poppies*

Holding on/ letting go

A poem dramatising the parental conflict between wanting to hold on to and protect one's children and the need to let them go and live their own lives, *Poppies* articulates every parent's worst fear - that their child may come to harm. And knowing this might be the case, of course, only makes the letting go even harder to bear.

Weir's poem is full of deliberately unclear time shifts. Time collapses, for instance, as the mother switches between memories of her son leaving to go to school and her son leaving to go to war. The speaker longs to hold on to her son, trying to turn back time so that the poem ends with her 'hoping to hear' her son's 'playground voice catching on the wind'. Time, the poem suggests, is fleeting. The wind, often a metaphor for elusiveness, clearly shows that both youth and memory are transitory and intangible; an idea that is particularly tragic in a poem so heavily dominated by physical textures and the senses. Whilst the alliteration of 'hoping to hear' captures how hard the mother strains to hear her son and recapture their close relationship from his childhood, we know that her attempts are futile.

Right from the start, the mother contrasts her personal loss with the grief of the nation. Repetition of 'before', in 'Three days before Armistice Sunday' and 'Before you left', highlights how precious the time before her son left was to the mother. The 'individual war graves', an ominous reminder of the cost of war, are juxtaposed with the distancing of the son from his mother as he leaves her. Here we see the first of numerous blurrings of time, as we are left to question whether the mother is remembering attaching a poppy to the schoolboy uniform of her child or to the 'blazer' of an adult soldier's dress uniform. The 'yellow bias binding' could signal either the smart finish on a school uniform, or the rank and regiment of a soldier. The metaphor of the 'blockade', however, is a clear, unambiguous sign of how the mother feels shut out of her son's life.

This 'binding' is part of the poem's semantic fields of imprisonment and liberation, key themes that run through the poem. There is a sense that perhaps the mother feels aggrieved by the military's 'binding' of her son to them, that she is secretly pleased to '[disrupt] a blockade' with her pinned poppy and stake her claim. However, we can also interpret this image as the complete opposite – that the pinning of the poppy, a symbol now irrevocably linked with the military, disrupts the 'yellow bias' of a blazer that reminds her of his childhood, representing the military's cutting of the ties between mother and son. It is just one of several ambiguous images within a poem that resists definitive interpretation.

Whilst the 'Sellotape bandaged around my hand' can be read as a metaphor for both the mother's emotional wounds and her son's potential future wounds, it also reflects how the mother's hands are figuratively tied. As much as she would like to keep her son within the domestic sphere and protect him, she cannot prevent him leaving. Nowhere is this clearer than in the third stanza, when separation finally takes places. Here, the 'front door' becomes a symbol of the dangerous outside world, a metaphor for the son's crossing of the boundary between the protected domestic and the unprotected public spheres. Unable to deny herself the opportunity to cling to their last few moments together, the mother congratulates herself for being 'brave, as I walked /with you, to the front door'. Her throwing open of the door is emotional, almost aggressive, emphasised by the sudden shift into rhyme, and forms a last challenge to the world that will take her son away. Her son shows less grief over their parting and is gone in a 'split second'. For him, the world is full of potential, 'overflowing /like a treasure chest', a simile that shows the excitement he feels at the freedom that awaits.

Like the 'song bird' the mother releases from the 'cage' in her son's bedroom, the son is free of the gilded cage of affection his mother has placed him in. It is no coincidence that the very next line describes how 'a single dove flew

from the pear tree': it is a clear metaphor for the son's liberation. Ancient Chinese mythology portrays the pear tree as a symbol of longevity and immortality; Weir appears to be implying that, whilst he has left the security of home for the more dangerous outside world, the son has achieved a measure of independence and freedom as shown by his 'single' status. Whilst the poem may end with the mother's hopeless straining to recapture her son's childhood, it also ends with her son free and unrestrained as the 'dove pulled freely against the sky'.

Inscriptions on the war memorial

As a textile designer, it is perhaps unsurprising that Weir roots much of *Poppies* in textures and physical contact. Much of the connection that the mother has with her son is expressed through tactile imagery, whether this comes from pinning the 'crimped petals' of a paper poppy to her son's lapel, removing cat hairs, or grazing noses in Eskimo kisses. For the mother, touch provides a physical connection that is stronger than memory and allows her to express her affection. Her memory of how she 'smoothed down your shirt's /upturned collar' is onomatopoeic; long double vowel sounds mimic her soothing, domestic motions and how much she cares. The 'gelled /blackthorns' of the son's hair, however, whilst also reminiscent of Christ's crown of thorns, are physical representations of the distance that grows between the mother and her son even before he leaves. Sharp and unwelcoming, the 'blackthorns' are a metaphor for how now the son has grown up; the mother is no longer able to freely touch him. With a relationship so heavily reliant on physical affection, it is perhaps to be expected that after the mother's touch is denied she complains that 'All my words /flattened, rolled, turned into felt'. With touch removed, the mother finds herself unable to fully articulate her emotions and communicate with her son, her voice crushed in a similar way to that of the felt used to make military caps.

The semantic field of textiles and sewing within the poem gives the mother a defined, domestic voice, emphasising her nurturing side through the allusions to the taking care of her son's clothes (and her son) over the years. The poem's early focus on the maintenance of her son's clothing – such as his 'blazer' and the 'upturned collar' of his shirt – provides a telling contrast to the later image of the mother being 'hat-less, without /a winter coat or reinforcements of scarf, gloves'. If clothing imagery reflects her bond with her son, it appears that without him the mother is left vulnerable and exposed. The military reference of 'reinforcements' only heightens this vulnerability, whilst also presenting us with the juxtaposition of the two worlds her son now belongs to. The mother seems increasingly consumed by anxiety over her son's fate: the image of her 'stomach busy /making tucks, darts, pleats' uses symbols of the domestic sphere to vividly depict her fears; the simple idea of a stomach knotted with anxiety transforms into striking imagery that almost tips into the realm of magical realism. Full of hard consonants and one-syllable words, the triple list mimics the sharp stabs of pain that accompany the mother's fear.

The continued use of sewing imagery only strengthens our understanding of the mother's fear in the final stanza, as she seeks to replace her lost physical bond with her son through the touching of objects she associates with him. The tracing of 'the inscriptions on the war memorial' allows her to form a tangible connection with her son, yet also hints at her fear that he too will someday end up carved upon it. The memorial's solidity contrasts distinctly with the imagery of the 'ornamental stitch' of the dove in the sky. A small but beautiful stitch, this image emphasises the fragility of her bond with her son and suggests that there is no longer any strong link between them; it also provides a visual reflection of her son's vulnerability and the dangers she sees in his apparent freedom.

Spasms of paper

Poppies is a poem with many semantic fields. As well as the previously explored fields of imprisonment/ liberation and textiles representing family conflict, the poem also features several references to injury and death. Opening with the ominous reminder of death through the mentions of Armistice Sunday and 'war graves', and ending in a church yard, the poem is saturated with subtle images of loss and violence, reflecting any parents' worst fears for their children. The poppy she pins to her son – already a famous symbol of loss thanks to John McCrae's poem *In Flanders Field* – is described as having 'crimped petals /spasms of paper red'. A powerful, emotive image that brings to mind extreme suffering, the 'spasms' suggest short bursts of severe pain (or perhaps even death throes), whilst the 'red' colouring has obvious associations with bloodshed.

Even the heavily domestic and caring imagery of the second stanza is stealthily infiltrated by the threat of violence. As previously mentioned, the choice to describe the mother's homemade Sellotape cat hair remover with the verb 'bandaged' provokes immediate associations with the treatment of injuries, perhaps comparing the mother's tender removal of cat hair with the treatment of the war injuries her son is likely to incur in the future. The innocent memory of Eskimo kisses shared 'when /you were little' is tainted by the desire to 'graze' her nose against his, once again linking to the poem's semantic field of injury. The 'gelled /blackthorns' of her son's hair, already a mournful image of the breaking down of familial bonds, has heavy religious connotations; alluding to the crucifixion of Christ, the 'blackthorns' imply that the son may be sacrificed for the greater good.

The fragility of the 'ornamental stitch' in the sky and the mother's tracing of the inscriptions of the dead leave the poem with an anxious tone of foreboding, a final image of a mother leaning against a war memorial 'like a wishbone', desperately praying for the return of her son to her safely. Though her son is still alive, she is keenly aware of his loss and mourns him – and his lost childhood – regardless.

As dismal a reading as this is, the poem can also be interpreted in a far more depressing way. As previously noted, *Poppies* is a complex poem that defies indisputable interpretation. Whilst the poem can be read as exploring a mother's sense of loss after her son grows up and goes to war, it must also be acknowledged that the poem also supports a reading where the son has died. The imagery of death could stem from the actual death of the son; the name the mother traces on the memorial could be her son's. The repeated imagery of doves, associated with peace, and birds in general can be read as symbolising the peace and freedom the son has achieved in death. In classical literature death is sometimes configured as birds taking flight; the dove's flight from the aforementioned pear tree perhaps works in this way to symbolise the loss of his life.

Regardless of the interpretation of the son's fate, *Poppies* is more than a poem about war. With its focus on emotion and loss, intertwined with the themes of memory and love, the poem develops a complex examination of the bond between mother and child and, specifically, or the emotional or psychological conflicts that can arise within this relationship.

Poppies crunched:

Before - poppies – graves – spasms – red – blockade – binding – bandaged – smoothed – upturned – graze – Eskimos - blackthorns – flattened – door – treasure – split – released – cage – single – dove – tucks – darts – pleats – traced – wishbone – freely – ornamental – stitch – playground – wind.

Beatrice Garland, *Kamikaze*

A horde of Mongol ships, hungry for destruction, led by the immortal Kublai Khan approaches the shores of Japan. Stranded and seeking a safe vantage from which to launch their attack they lie in wait. A matter of time. Nature, a force in Japan so often malevolent and so often injudicious was, however, to intervene. And its intervention was decisive.

The vengeful 1281 typhoon that swept the Mongols from the sea was christened a kamikaze or 'divine wind.' The Mongols were never to attack Japan again.

Although the Mongol fleet was never to be seen again, the sound of the divine wind was to echo through the history of Japan. It whistled through the air towards the American ships as they massed in the water around Japan, it was to be heard in the deafening detonation of the atomic bombs over Nagasaki and Hiroshima and in the poem *Kamikaze* by Beatrice Garland.

Garland once said she would 'spend a lot of the day listening to other people's worlds'. This secret ear for the inner workings and motivations of others is the skill that allows her to unpick the 'powerful incantations' that drive the poem's principal character, the pilot, towards the sea. The poem hints at clues that led to the entanglement of self-destruction and honour: 'a samurai sword', a 'huge flag waved' and 'little fishing boats'. Each image presents the three conflicting drives in the mind of the pilot. The sword is symbolic of the Bushido code of honour, a simple life and self-sacrifice, the flag in its infinite waving loop references a deep unfathomable patriotism and the fishing boats evoke the pastoral beauty and oceanic tradition of the paintings of Hokusai.

If an 'incantation' is a powerful pattern of phrase repeated again and again, then these images of honour, tradition and loyalty have been repeated often throughout the history of Japan. Like the poem their message has passed from generation to generation leaving its lasting imprint. The children in the poem 'learn' from a process of emotional osmosis and become a simulacrum of their parents. As the lines and stanzas enjamb into each other so too do the attitudes as they are passed onwards.

What we are led then to question is what is the real weapon in the poem: the destructive potential of the Kamikaze pilot or the 'incantations' that send him plunging towards the sea, the divine wind come once again to save Japan from the aggressor. Neither? And what is true bravery here? To sacrifice your life unthinkingly for emperor or country, or to go against indoctrination and face down the bitter scorn of society?

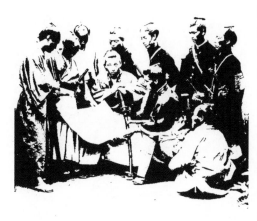

The rich 'Bushido' or Samurai tradition of self-sacrifice, loyalty and simple life inspire awe rather than revulsion as, very often, has the destructive power of the seas (take a look at Hokusai's *The Wave*). So, what is being criticised in the poem? Why are we meant to empathise with the pilot, why 'must' we feel his emotions as he performs his noble and yet devastating sacrifice? Much like Tennyson's *The Charge of the Light Brigade*

or Hughes' *Bayonet Charge* the poem functions as a critique of the propaganda that piggybacked on venerable traditions. The chance to become a Kamikaze offers a 'one-way journey into history'. Here we see the classic diction of propaganda. The semantic field of adventure tells us this is a fairy story that has been sold to these men in order that they so willingly 'embark[ed]' on their 'journey'. Yet the pilot loses no dignity in the opening stanza when he carries his 'samurai sword' as if he is some spiritual successor to the noble Bushido. Yet this young man is only sent with 'enough' fuel for a one-way trip. The juxtaposition of his youth and sense of adventure cuts sharply against the deadly fuel allowance of the regime who have cruelly counted out his remaining time on earth out in aviation fuel. They certainly aren't accounting for the pilot's ultimate decision to return home. Returning as he does, despite the half empty tank, adds a sense of defiance and a different kind of bravery to the one traditionally expected by the parents who greet him on his return.

An ear for other worlds

Stanza two again emphasises the ear we need for the worlds of others. We, and the persona's children, are asked to believe that he 'must' have looked down upon the sea. And the sea, so pivotal in the life of an island nation, in this story reflects flashes of his own life before his eyes. The 'dark shoals' of fish become figurative for the 'flag' which in itself reflects his own indecision being 'waved one way, then the  other'; the little boats become a fragment of childhood 'bunting' or perhaps the memory of a military parade while the 'flashing silver' of the tuna are the kamikaze who fly with him.

It is these same pilots who are the 'brothers' referenced in stanza three. The 'cairns' they built are ancient markers; it could suggest that his 'brothers' followed the traditional, 'ancient' mindset, and that he is the exception; one who values his own individualism in the face of death. Yet we could also look at these 'cairns' as metaphors for withstanding the 'turbulent inrushes' and impulse to war and destruction. However, we view them, we have to read a critique of the prevailing wisdom of the time. The stanza lacks punctuation and in itself becomes an 'incantation' to cherishing life. The infinite loop ∞ of the flag, representing the perpetual cycle of war and destruction, is rejected and replaced with the sibilant sounds of the ocean and ever onrushing waves. The pilot returns to land like everything else, 'shore, salt-sodden...awash' and yet also remarkably colourful. 'Crabs', 'mackerel', 'prawns' which are 'butt marked' and 'feathery'. Amongst this plethora of life affirming imagery and debris from the sea the pilot is returned to land '-safe', his bounty hanging like decorative medals.

Reborn, the hero returns to the shore. He has fought off the 'breakers' of predominant wisdom, turned from the infinite cycle of destruction and defied the half-empty tank he was sent on his 'journey' with. Yet he is now a 'dark prince... dangerous' a negative influence to be shunned. The semantic field of shame tells us of a culture that isn't ready to accept this new form of anti-conformist heroism. The defiance of the older generation eventually seeps through to the young who too avoid their grandfather as 'chatter' and

'laughter' turns to 'silence'. It seems clear, that we, as readers, are being asked to scorn the parents whose attitudes are thrown into sharp contrast with the colourful man who emerges from the sea. Thus the 'silence' at the end of the poem is remarkably free from any form of condemnation and an opportunity for the reader to make up their own mind, unlike the children who had it made for them.

Of course, the cycle of destruction, like a great wave, will pass over one man. The bombs that fell on Japan in 1945 were another destructive and divine wind. The controversial shrines or 'cairns' that pay homage to the bravery of the kamikaze are still visited in droves by tourists. What then is the message of the poem? It is illusive in many respects and problematised by the fact that we will never truly know what caused the pilot to abandon his mission. Was it the visions of beauty; the endless wealth of the ocean? Or was it cowardice? This distance is highlighted by the third person perspective we get in the first stanzas. This perspective is full of colour and imagery and when we finally switch to the first person the language becomes solemn, almost shameful of the act of shaming itself.

Kamikaze crunched:

Embarked – samurai – shaven – powerful – one-way – history – half – children – looked – little – strung – sea – arcing – flag – eight – dark – flashing – sun – remembered – waiting – cairns – withstood – turbulent – father's – grandfather's – awash – cloud-marked – black – silver – dangerous – back – mother – eyes – neighbours – existed – children – learned – silent – returned – loved – wondered – die.

Teaching & revision ideas

1. As you know, the exam task is a comparative essay on two of these poems. To help prepare for this task, write down the name of each poem on a separate piece of paper. Turn the pieces of paper over so that you cannot see which one is which. Now turn over three pieces of paper at random. Your task to discuss how two of these poems are similar and how one of them is different to the other two. Once you've exhausted your comparative skills return the pieces to the pack, pick another three and start the process again. This task can be completed individually or in pairs.

2. There's no better way to appreciate the skills involved in writing a dramatic monologue or a sonnet than by having a go yourself. Write the Count's letter back to The Duke from Browning's poem in the form of rhymed verse. Alternatively try rewriting Browning's poem in the form of a sonnet. Writing back would also work well with Agard's poem, *Checking Out Me History*. What might his teachers write back to him?

3. Visual stimuli can be great ways of introducing poems, especially those rich in visual imagery. *War Photographer*, for instance, could be introduced via the famous image of children suffering from a Napalm attack in the Vietnam war.

4. A relatively long poem such as the extract from Wordsworth's *The Prelude* can be broken down and made accessible in many different ways. For this poem, we'd be inclined to introduce it to a class through lexico-semantic fields and play a game we call 'Linguistic Detectives'. Separate words or phrases from the poem into distinct categories. Put the class into a number of small groups. Each group is given first one and then another of the categories. Their task is to work out what the words in their category have in common – the similarity could be

grammatical, i.e. they're all adjectives, or lexical, i.e. they are all complex Latinate words. As in all detective stories they should also be alert to any words that don't fit the pattern, clues that are red herrings. Once they've spent around five minutes on this you can add the second set of clues, or category of words. This time they follow the same process but also need to try to link the two categories together. From their deductions they should try to write a number of statements about what they think the poem might be about and when it might have been written. Each group can then read out their words and statements to the rest of the class. Once this exercise is complete give them a few minutes to pull the now complete set of clues together and to speculate about the poem. In practice, usually this means that the class, or most of them perhaps, are more than usually interested in reading the poem to discover how accurate they were. Here are some suggested word groupings for *The Prelude*:

Category 1: boat, cove, oars, chain, shove, pinnace, elfin

Category 2: grim. huge, power, towered, mighty, craggy, purpose, darkness

Category 3: black, undetermined, dim, unknown, covert, silent, desertion, no, blank

Category 4: mind, dreams, sense, view, mood, brain, thoughts, heaving

Category 5: summit, boundary, horizon, ridge, utmost, unswerving, bound

Category 6: stars, sparkling, glittering, grey, sky, light, moon, melted.

5. Encouraging discerning evaluation of poetry is key to developing pupils' critical awareness. Individually, or in pairs pupils, could list the poems as a top ten, excluding five poems from the list. Once a top ten has been shared with a class each individual, or pair, can argue to change one poem's position and substitute one of the remaining five poems for one in the top ten. And so on around the class.

6. Use the grid on the next page to help visualise and keep track of contrasts and comparisons:

Comparison Grid

	Power of Humans	Power of Nature	Power of Conflict	Effects of Conflict	Reality of Conflict	Loss and Absence	Memory	Anger	Guilt	Fear	Pride	Identity	Individual Experience
Ozymandias													
London													
The Prelude: Stealing the Boat													
My Last Duchess													
The Charge of the Light Brigade													
Exposure													
Storm on the Island													
Bayonet Charge													
Remains													
Poppies													
War Photographer													
Tissue													
The Emigree													
Kamikaze													
Checking Out Me History													

Comparing the poems

As we indicated in the introduction, the best comparisons arise from choosing texts that have strong differences as well as similarities. Texts that are too similar or too different make the task much more difficult. Although these poems obviously share the broad theme of power and conflict, as we've discovered, they explore very different types of power and conflict and approach the topic in a wide range of ways. Some of the poems can easily be paired with each other and we suggest you try to match each one up with at 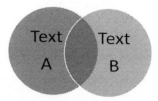 least one other poem before you consider our suggested pairings. This list is, of course, not exhaustive and some of the pairings would make for easier comparison than others.

Clearly there's a group of poems that explore warfare and all of these work well with each other as there are contrasts as well as similarities. **The Charge of Light Brigade** and **Bayonet Charge**, for instance, both describe the visceral experience of fighting. Indeed Hughes' poem could almost be read as a response to Tennyson's; whereas Tennyon's cavalry are driven, according to the poet, by patriotic fervour, patriotic feelings are 'dropped like luxuries' by Hughes' single soldier; whereas Tennyson claims the cavalry accept their duty and sacrifice willingly, Hughes's soldier is stripped of everything except the urgent will to survive. Armitage's **Remains** also explores conflict and, like Hughes' poem focuses on a single character's experience. Though both poets take us into the minds and feelings of their characters, Armtiage is more interested in the psychological aftermath of violence. Telling comparisons could, of course, also be made between *The Charge of the Light Brigade* and Owen's **Exposure**, unsurprising as Owen wrote explicitly about his desire to convey the 'pity of war'. The main enemy in *Exposure* is nature itself a fact would allow interesting comparison with Hughes' poem where nature appears to suffer collateral damage.

As we have seen, the relationships between man and nature was a central preoccupation of Romantic poets. Owen's poem borrows motifs from Romanticism, but reverses the semantic polarity. For example, 'dawn' in Romanticism is used consistently as a symbol of hope and new beginnings. In *Exposure*, however, it is amassing an army to attack the soldiers. Depciting conflict been man and nature, Owen's poem could be compared interestingly with **Ozymandias**, the extract from **The Prelude** and with Blake's **London**, the latter of which also shares Owen's sense of witness and protest against injustice. The abuse of power is also central to both *London* and the despotic *Ozymandias*. Heaney's **Station Island** is a more modern poem that also explores the elemental conflict between humans and the environment.

Remains and *Exposure* share a focus on the impact of warfare or violence on soldiers. Duffy's **War Photographer** is also interested in how its protagonist copes with their traumatic experiences. Like *Remains* there is a strong sense of separation of this character from the rest of society and of being trapped by and in their own memories. Memory is, of course, central too to Wordsworth's Prelude in which one particular incident sticks in the poet's troubled mind and haunts his dreams. The separation and hostility Duffy's protagonist feels towards society links it to Agard's **Checking Out Me History** where the poem's speaker angrily rejects the stories he has been fed and embraces alternative stories that have been suppressed. Agard's angry protest connects him across time with Blake.

Conflicts between individuals and society feature prominently in the anthology; Garland's **Kamikaze** also springs to mind. At other times this conflict becomes more internal and psychological, as in Rumens' **Emigree**, a poem about idenity, like *The Prelude* and *Checking Out*. At other times this conflict is shrunk down to the scale of family relationships and those betwen men and women as in Weir's **Poppies** and Browning's **My Last Duchess**. Browning's poem is a dramatic monologue, i.e. it is written in the voice of a character, as is Armitage's *Remains*. Like Armitage's, Browning's poem presents itself as neat, orderly and controlled. Only on closer examination do we discover the disorder and violence that this impression belies. Heaney's

Station Island shares this outer appearance of robustnessand an interior more disturbed by the conflicts the poem dramatises. Though it is not a dramatic monologue, Agard's poem has a very strong sense of the speaking voice and, like Armitage's, is expressed in an idiom that diverges significantly from Standard English.

Of course, you will be able to make many more links. You could, for instance, consider other poems that are primarily driven by sonic imagery or those constructed through the visual dimension. Or you might group poems that share similar emotions or tones. We, however, haven't the space or time to do this. Perhaps the hardest poem to compare with others in the cluster is Dharker's **Tissue**. To some extent the theme of this poem could be read as the conflict between values in society with the poet proposing that society needs to be constructed around human values. This individual/ society conflict links Dharker's poem to *London*, *War Photographer*, *Checking Out*, *Emigree* and *Kamikaze*. Perhaps, though, a more interesting and certainly more unusual comparison would be through the imagery employed by Dharker. In particular, the visual focus on light connects it to *Emigree* and the prominent tactile imagery could be compared with how it is used in Weir's *Poppies*.

Knowledge→ Understanding→ Appreciation

Developing appreciation about how poetry works and how the poems in the AQA anthology work takes time and effort. Pupils need to develop a good grounding first about poetry and on each of these poems. Given time and encouragement, from this knowledge understanding will spring. Exercises that encourage discussion, debate and creative engagement with poetry, such as having a go at writing a poem, will help pupils make the critical leap from understanding to appreciation. And appreciation is the key to top level critical essays.

A relatively fun way to develop knowledge is, of course, through quizzes. So here's some sample questions. Some are fairly straightforward and a few a little more tricky...

Part 1: Content of the anthology poems

1. How many soldiers rode in *Charge of the Light Brigade*?
2. Which poem is the only example of a sonnet in the cluster?
3. What is the name of the artist referred to in *My Last Duchess*?
4. What does the poetic voice hear within the cries of every voice in *London*? "Mind-forged _____"
5. What punctuation mark is used within the first line of *Storm on the Island* after the first clause?
6. How many syllables does each line have within *The Prelude*?
7. What is frequently personified within *Exposure*?
8. Which three poems are written with the poetic voice of a solider?
9. A "stranger's features" are described in War Photographer as "a half-formed_____"
10. Which poems deviate from Standard English?

Part 2: Contexts in which the anthology poems were written

10.   Which war is *COTLB* set in?
11.   Who did Simon Armitage interview to gain material for the poem *Remains* and others in the collection?

12.   *Poppies* was written as a response to the losses suffered during the wars in which two countries?

13.   What historical event inspired Percy Shelley's political views?

14.   What does the word *Kamikaze* mean in Japanese?

15.   Which Guyanan poet explores the theme of cultural identity in much of his work?

16.   In which period in literature was Blake an important figure?

Part 3: Subject terminology

17.   What is the repetition of the first consonant sound in words called?

18.   What is the repetition of vowel sounds in the middle of words called?

19.   What is a a comparison of two different things using the words like or as called?

20.   Giving human traits to non-living things is called what?

21.   What is the term for when words imitate the sounds associated with the objects or actions they refer to?

22.   What is the name for a comparison between two things which does NOT include like or as?

23.   What is the term for a regular number of beats per line in a poem?

24.   Name three different forms of poems.

25.   What is the difference between metre and rhythm?

NB

Answers to this quiz and to the following task can be found on our literature website, peripeteia.webs.com

Terminology task

The following is a list of poetry terminology and short definitions of the terms. Unfortunately, cruel, malicious individuals (i.e. us) have scrambled them up. Your task is to unscramble the list, matching each term to the correct definition. Good luck!

Term	Definition
Imagery	Vowel rhyme, e.g. 'bat' and 'lag'
Metre	An implicit comparison in which one thing is said to be
Rhythm	another
Simile	Description in poetry
Metaphor	A conventional metaphor, such as a 'dove' for peace
Symbol	A metrical foot comprising an unstressed followed by a
Iambic	stressed beat
Pentameter	A line with five beats
Enjambment	Description in poetry using metaphor, simile or
Caesura	personification
Dramatic monologue	A repeated pattern of ordered sound
Figurative imagery	An explicit comparison of two things, using 'like' or 'as'
Onomatopoeia	Words, or combinations of words, whose sounds mimic
Lyric	their meaning
Adjective	Words in a line starting with the same letter or sound
Alliteration	A strong break in a line, usually signalled by punctuation
Ballad	A regular pattern of beats in each line
Sonnet	A narrative poem with an alternating four and three beat
Assonance	line
Sensory imagery	A word that describes a noun
Quatrain	A 14 line poem following a number of possible rhyme
Diction	schemes
Personification	When a sentence steps over the end of a line and
	continues into the next line or stanza
	Description that uses the senses
	A four line stanza
	Inanimate objects given human characteristics
	A poem written in the voice of a character
	A poem written in the first person, focusing on the
	emotional experience of the narrator
	A term to describe the vocabulary used in a poem.

A sonnet of revision activities

1. Reverse millionaire: 10,000 points if students can guess the poem just from one word from it. You can vary the difficulty as much as you like. For example, 'clams', would be fairly easily identifiable as from Sexton's poem whereas 'fleet' would be more difficult. 1000 points if students can name the poem from a single phrase or image – 'portion out the stars and dates'. 100 points for a single line. 10 points for recognising the poem from a stanza. Play individually or in teams.

2. Research the poet. Find one sentence about them that you think sheds light on their poem in the anthology. Compare with your classmates. Or find a couple more lines or a stanza by a poet and see if others can recognise the writer from their lines.

3. Write a cento based on one or more of the poems. A cento is a poem constructed from lines from other poems. Difficult, creative, but also fun, perhaps.

4. Read 3 or 4 other poems by one of the poets. Write a pastiche. See if classmates can recognise the poet you're imitating.

5. Write the introduction for a critical guide on the poems aimed at next year's yr. 10 class.

6. Use the poet Glynn Maxwell's typology of poems to arrange the poems into different groups. In his excellent book, *On Poetry*, Maxwell suggests poems have four dominant aspects, which he calls solar, lunar, musical and visual. A solar poem hits home, is immediately striking. A lunar poem, by contrast, is more mysterious and might not give up its meanings so easily. Ideally a lunar poem will haunt your imagination. Written mainly for the ear, a musical poem focuses on the sounds of language, rather than the meanings. Think of Lewis Carroll's

Jabberwocky. A visual poem is self-conscious about how it looks to the eye. Concrete poems are the ultimate visual poems. According to Maxwell, the very best poems are strong in each dimension. Try applying this test to each poem. Which ones come out on top?

7. Maxwell also recommends conceptualising the context in which the words of the poem are created or spoken. Which poems would suit being read around a camp fire? Which would be better declaimed from the top of a tall building? Which might you imagine on a stage? Which ones are more like conversation overheard? Which are the easiest and which the most difficult to place?

8. Mr Maxwell is a fund of interesting ideas. He suggests all poems dramatise a battle between the forces of whiteness and blackness, nothingness and somethingness, sound and silence, life and death. In each poem, what is the dynamic between whiteness and blackness? Which appears to have the upper hand?

9. Still thinking in terms of evaluation, consider the winnowing effect of time. Which of the modern poems do you think might be still read in 20, a 100 or 200 years? Why?

10. Give yourself only the first and last line of one of the poems. Without peeking at the original, try to fill in the middle. Easy level: write in prose. Expert level: attempt verse.

11. According to Russian Formalist critics, poetry performs a 'controlled explosion on ordinary language'. What evidence can you find in this selection of controlled linguistic detonations?

12. A famous musician once said that though he wasn't the best at playing all the notes, nobody played the silences better. In Japanese garden water features the sound of a water drop is designed to make us notice the silence around it. Try reading one of the poems in the light of these

comments, focusing on the use of white space, caesuras, punctuation – all the devices that create the silence on which the noise of the poem rests.

13. In *Notes on the Art of Poetry*, Dylan Thomas wrote that 'the best craftsmanship always leaves holes and gaps in the works of the poem so that something that is not in the poem can creep, crawl, flash or thunder in'. Examine a poem in the light of this comment, looking for its holes and gaps. If you discover these, what 'creeps', 'crawls' or 'flashes' in to fill them?

14. Different types of poems conceive the purpose of poetry differently. Broadly speaking Augustan poets of the eighteenth century aimed to impress their readers with the wit of their ideas and the elegance of the expression. In contrast, Romantic poets wished to move their readers' hearts. Characteristically Victorian poets aimed to teach the readers some kind of moral principle or example. Self-involved, avant-garde Modernists weren't overly bothered about finding, never mind pleasing, a general audience. What impact do the AQA anthology poems seek? Do they seek to amuse, appeal to the heart, teach us something? Are they like soliloquies – the overheard inner workings of thinking – or more like speeches or mini-plays? Try placing each poem somewhere on the following continuums. Then create a few continuums of your own. As ever, comparison with your classmates will prove illuminating.

Emotional..intellectual
Feelings..ideas
Internal..external
Contemplative...rhetorical
Open..guarded

Guess who

In this demanding revision task students should try to match the following extracts to the poets who feature in the anthology. If you want an even sterner test, mix in a few other poems. Once students have matched the poems they could write short explanations of how they arrived at their deductions. This might include comments on diction, idiom, imagery, metre, form and so on.

Extract 1.

Not a red rose or a satin heart.

I give you an onion.
It is a moon wrapped in brown paper.
It promises light
like the careful undressing of love

2.

Move him into the sun—
Gently its touch awoke him once,
At home, whispering of fields half-sown.
Always it woke him, even in France,
Until this morning and this snow.
If anything might rouse him now
The kind old sun will know.

3.

Here, in this strange place,
In a disjointed time,
I am nothing but a space
That someone has to fill.
Images invade me.

4.

Against the rubber tongues of cows and the hoeing hands of men
Thistles spike the summer air
And crackle open under a blue-black pressure.

5.

Every Night & every Morn
Some to Misery are Born
Every Morn and every Night
Some are Born to sweet delight
Some are Born to sweet delight
Some are Born to Endless Night.

6.

The men lie, abstract shapes & sizes
angled & shattered in beds,
a fraction between types & ages.

7.

O wild West Wind, thou breath of Autumn's being,
Thou, from whose unseen presence the leaves dead
Are driven, like ghosts from an enchanter fleeing,

Yellow, and black, and pale, and hectic red,
Pestilence-stricken multitudes

8.

It's cold, you say, the house.
Yes, of courses I'll go back one day,
Visit, that is. But the house

Will be cold, just as you say.

9.

It looked like a clump of small dusty nettles
Growing wild at the gable of the house
Beyond where we dumped our refuse and old bottles:
Unverdant ever, almost beneath notice.

10.

He is not here; but far away
    The noise of life begins again,
    And ghastly thro' the drizzling rain
On the bald street breaks the blank day.

11.

Fair seed-time had my soul, and I grew up
Fostered alike by beauty and by fear.

12.

Explain yuself
wha yu mean
when yu say half-caste
yu mean when picasso
mix red an green
is a half-caste canvas?

13.

Batman, big shot, when you gave the order
to grow up, then let me loose to wander
leeward, freely through the wild blue yonder
as you liked to say, or ditched me, rather

14.

Today, a rare openness
to the edge in all events:
the way good things can hurt
with the sharpness of a blade.
Take love for example

15.

In one long yellow string I wound
    Three times her little throat around,
And strangled her.

Critical soundbites

Another demanding, but rewarding revision activity. This time students must match the following excerpts from criticism to the poet whose work they describe. [As with Guess the poet, the answers are at the end of this book].

1. This poet's 'vision embraces radical subjects such as poverty, child labour and abuse, the repressive nature of state and church, as well as right of children to be treated as individuals with their own desires'.

2. 'Others have shown the disenchantment of war, have unlegended the roselight and romance of it, but none with such compassion for the disenchanted nor such sternly just and justly stern judgment on the idyllisers.'

3. The poet's themes include 'language and the representation of reality; the construction of the self; gender issues; contemporary culture; and many different forms of alienation, oppression and social inequality'.

4. This poet 'explores what she calls her 'real country': 'movement, transition, crossing over', as well as the tensions between secular and religious cultures in a world of fear and emergent fundamentalisms'.

5. Their poetry 'displays an array of social, historical, political and emotional preoccupations, worrying at its themes with a diverse range of scenarios, situations and voices'.

6. In their 'blend of puckish wit, social observation and playful humour, these poems often revel in disrupting the establishment and accepted opinion'.

7. As a poet, 'he was always at his best while struggling to become a whole person, to reconcile the sense of incoherence and disappointment forced upon him by time and circumstance with those intimations of harmonious communion promised by his childhood visions'.

8. 'As official poetic spokesman for the reign of Victoria, he felt called upon to celebrate a quickly changing industrial and mercantile world with which he felt little in common, for his deepest sympathies were called forth by an unaltered rural England.'

9. This poet's 'work is marked by a mythical framework, using the lyric and dramatic monologue to illustrate intense subject matter'.

10. The major themes are there in this poet's 'dramatic if short life and in his works, enigmatic, inspiring, and lasting: the restlessness and brooding, the rebellion against authority, the interchange with nature, the power of the visionary imagination and of poetry, the pursuit of ideal love, and the untamed spirit ever in search of freedom'.

11. 'Poetry is a way of talking about how each of us sees, is touched by, grasps, and responds to our own different worlds and the people in them.'

12. Their poems 'possess a vitality...a heightened chattiness that combines idiomatic cliché with arresting and often unusual observations and descriptions, spanning his favoured territory of tall tales, humorous dramatic monologues and often sinister, noirish anecdotes.'

13. He won the Nobel Prize for Literature in 1995 "for works of lyrical beauty and ethical depth, which exalt everyday miracles and the living past".

14. 'Their subject is dramatic personae, men and women. There never was for this poet any other subject.'

15. The subjects of 'their own poetry are often unapologetically those of femininity and the domains of domesticity (Anne Stevenson has described them as a writer 'who retains her feminine voice but extends her sympathies beyond feminism').

GLOSSARY

ALLITERATION – the repetition of consonants at the start of neighbouring words in a line

ANAPAEST - a three beat pattern of syllables, unstress, unstress, stress. E.g. 'on the moon', 'to the coast', 'anapaest'

ANTITHESIS - the use of balanced opposites

APOSTROPHE – a figure of speech addressing a person, object or idea

ASSONANCE – vowel rhyme, e.g. sod and block

BLANK VERSE – unrhymed lines of iambic pentameter

BLAZON – a male lover describing the parts of his beloved

CADENCE – the rise of fall of sounds in a line of poetry

CAESURA – a distinct break in a poetic line, usually marked by punctuation

COMPLAINT – a type of love poem concerned with loss and mourning

CONCEIT – an extended metaphor

CONSONANCE – rhyme based on consonants only, e.g. book and back

COUPLET – a two line stanza, conventionally rhyming

DACTYL – the reverse pattern to the anapaest; stress, unstress, unstress. E.g. 'Strong as a'

DRAMATIC MONOLOGUE – a poem written in the voice of a distinct character

ELEGY – a poem in mourning for someone dead

END-RHYME – rhyming words at the end of a line

END-STOPPED – the opposite of enjambment; i.e. when the sentence and the poetic line stop at the same point

ENJAMBMENT – where sentences run over the end of lines and stanzas

FIGURATIVE LANGUAGE – language that is not literal, but employs figures of speech, such as metaphor, simile and personification

FEMININE RHYME – a rhyme that ends with an unstressed syllable or unstressed syllables.

FREE VERSE – poetry without metre or a regular, set form

GOTHIC – a style of literature characterised by psychological horror, dark deeds and uncanny events

HEROIC COUPLETS – pairs of rhymed lines in iambic pentameter

HYPERBOLE – extreme exaggeration

IAMBIC – a metrical pattern of a weak followed by a strong stress, ti-TUM, like a heart beat

IMAGERY – the umbrella term for description in poetry. Sensory imagery refers to descriptions that appeal to sight, sound and so forth; figurative imagery refers to the use of devices such as metaphor, simile and personification

JUXTAPOSITION – two things placed together to create a strong contrast

LYRIC – an emotional, personal poem usually with a first person speaker

MASCULINE RHYME – an end rhyme on a strong syllable

METAPHOR – an implicit comparison in which one thing is said to be another

METAPHYSICAL – a type of poetry characterised by wit and extended metaphors

METRE – the regular pattern organising sound and rhythm in a poem

MOTIF – a repeated image or pattern of language, often carrying thematic significance

OCTET OR OCTAVE – the opening eight lines of a sonnet

ONOMATOPOEIA – bang, crash, wallop

PENTAMETER – a poetic line consisting of five beats

PERSONIFICATION – giving human characteristics to inanimate things

PLOSIVE – a type of alliteration using 'p' and 'b' sounds

QUATRAIN – a four-line stanza

REFRAIN – a line or lines repeated like a chorus

ROMANTIC – A type of poetry characterised by a love of nature, by strong emotion and heightened tone

SESTET – the last six lines in a sonnet

SIMILE – an explicit comparison of two different things

SONNET – a form of poetry with fourteen lines and a variety of possible set rhyme patterns

SPONDEE – two strong stresses together in a line of poetry

STANZA – the technical name for a verse

SYMBOL – something that stands in for something else. Often a concrete representation of an idea.

SYNTAX – the word order in a sentence. doesn't Without sense English syntax make. Syntax is crucial to sense: For example, though it uses all the same words, 'the man eats the fish' is not the same as 'the fish eats the man'

TERCET – a three-line stanza

TETRAMETER – a line of poetry consisting of four beats

TROCHEE – the opposite of an iamb; stress, unstress, strong, weak.

VILLANELLE – a complex interlocking verse form in which lines are recycled

VOLTA – the 'turn' in a sonnet from the octave to the sestet

Recommended reading

Atherton, C. & Green, A. Teaching English Literature 16-19. NATE, 2013

Bate, J. Ted Hughes, The Unauthorised Life. William Collins, 2016

Bowen et al. The Art of Poetry, vol.1-4. Peripeteia Press, 2015-16

Brinton, I. Contemporary Poetry. CUP, 2009

Eagleton, T. How to Read a Poem. Wiley & Sons, 2006

Fry, S. The Ode Less Travelled. Arrow, 2007

Hamilton, I. & Noel-Todd, J. Oxford Companion to Modern Poetry, OUP, 2014

Heaney, S. The Government of the Tongue. Farrar, Straus & Giroux, 1976

Herbert, W. & Hollis, M. Strong Words. Bloodaxe, 2000

Howarth, P. The Cambridge Introduction to Modernist Poetry. CUP, 2012

Hurley, M. & O'Neill, M. Poetic Form, An Introduction. CUP, 2012

Meally, M. & Bowen, N. The Art of Writing English Literature Essays, Peripeteia Press, 2014

Maxwell, G. On Poetry. Oberon Masters, 2012

Padel, R. 52 Ways of Looking at a Poem. Vintage, 2004

Padel, R. The Poem and the Journey. Vintage, 2008

Paulin, T. The Secret Life of Poems. Faber & Faber, 2011

Quinn, J. The Cambridge Introduction to Modern Irish Poetry, CUP, 2008

Schmidt, M. Lives of the Poets, Orion, 1998

Wolosky, S. The Art of Poetry: How to Read a Poem. OUP, 2008.

About the authors

Head of English and freelance writer, Neil Bowen has a Masters Degree in Literature & Education from Cambridge University and is a member of Ofqual's experts panel for English. He is the author of *The Art of Writing English Essays for GCSE*, co-author of *The Art of Writing English Essays for A-level and Beyond* and of *The Art of Poetry*, volumes 1-5. Neil runs the peripeteia project, bridging the gap between A-level and degree level English courses: www.peripeteia.webs.com.

Karen Elson is an English teacher with a Masters degree in English Literature from Cardiff University.

Kathrine Mortimore is a Lead Practitioner at Torquay Academy. She has a Masters degree in Advanced Subject Teaching from Cambridge University where she focused on tackling disadvantage in the English classroom, a topic she has continued to blog about at: kathrinemortimore.wordpress.com

Neil Jones is an English teacher with a PhD in English Literature from Oxford University, where he specialised in modern poetry.

Answers to Guess the poet

1. Duffy, *Valentine*
2. Owen, *Futility*
3. Dharker, *Postcards from God 1*
4. Hughes, *Thistles*
5. Blake, *Auguries of Innocence*
6. Weir, *1916, Working With Red In a Field Hospital, Belgium*
7. Shelley, *Ode to the West Wind*
8. Rumens, *From a Conversation During Divorce*
9. Heaney, *Mint*
10. Tennyson, *In Memoriam*
11. Wordsworth, *The Prelude*
12. Agard, *Half-Caste*
13. Armitage, *Batman*
14. Garland, *The Vineyard*
15. Browning, *Porphyria's Lover*

Answers to critical soundbites

1. Blake
2. Owen
3. Rumens
4. Dharker
5. Weir
6. Agard
7. Wordsworth
8. Tennyson
9. Hughes
10. Shelley
11. Garland
12. Armitage
13. Browning
14. Heaney
15. Duffy

A final revision task: Students create their own anonymised critical sound bites. The class have to match the sound bite to the poet/ poem.

Critical sound bites adapted from:

https://literature.britishcouncil.org
http://www.warpoets.org
http://www.poetryfoundation.org
http://www.theguardian.com
https://www.bl.uk/collection-items/william-blakes-songs-of-innocence-and-experience
http://www.poetryarchive.org

9356127R00091

Printed in Germany
by Amazon Distribution
GmbH, Leipzig